REG REAGAN

This is My Life!

THERE'S MORE TO LIFE THAN BIFF

REG REAGAN

This is My Life!

MACMILLAN
Pan Macmillan Australia

First published 2004 in Macmillan by Pan Macmillan Australia Pty Limited
St Martins Tower, 31 Market Street, Sydney

Copyright © Matthew Johns 2004

All rights reserved. No part of this book may be reproduced or transmitted in any form or by any means, electronic, mechanical, including photocopying, recording or by any information storage and retrieval system, without prior permission in writing from the publisher.

National Library of Australia
Cataloguing-in-Publication data:

Johns, Matthew.
This is my life!: there's more to life than biff

ISBN 1 4050 3609 5.

1. Johns, Matthew – Characters – Reg Reagan. 2. Footy show (Television program). 3. Football players – Australia – Humour. 4. Rugby League football – Australia – Humour. I. Title.

796.3338092

Set in 13/16 pt AGaramond by Post Pre-press Group
Printed in Australia by McPherson's Printing Group
Internal illustrations by Bland Design
Pages 2, 120, 142, 169: Bill Green
Page 155: AAP
Pages 7, 12, 75 and 186: Getty Images
Page 68: Newspix

Papers used by Pan Macmillan Australia Pty Ltd are natural, recyclable products made from wood grown in sustainable forests. The manufacturing processes conform to the environmental regulations of the country of origin.

Contents

1	Sprung!	1
2	The Making of Me	6
3	The Reagan Bunch	11
4	Reg Reagan, Boy Wonder	19
5	Pecking Order	25
6	Wiped Out	33
7	The Price of Genius	44
8	Captain America	54
9	Sacked	62
10	Bring Back the Bush	67
11	Family Man	74
12	Baggy Green Gut	79
13	The Legendary Double	94
14	Rugby League Warrior	119
15	How I Won the Comp	127
16	Hello, World – It's Reg Reagan!	141
17	A Night at the Oprah	149
18	The Education of Bobby De Niro	154
19	Turfed Out	168
20	A Man Among Men	185
21	This Was My Life	211

1
SPRUNG!

THIS MIGHT SURPRISE YOU, but I love a drink and a chat. Every Wednesday afternoon I meet up with some old mates at a pub in Sydney's Surry Hills to sink a quick dozen schooners. We catch up on what's happening around the traps and swap stories about my legendary life and sporting prowess. One day not so long ago, after a few hours drinking and chatting, it was time for me to leave for my regular appointment at A Touch Of Class massage and relaxation centre in nearby Riley Street. A Touch Of Class, you understand, is the place I go to have any soreness or muscle tightness treated.

The girls there have magic in their fingers and know how to rub those aches and tension away. They massage you from head to toe and find every nook and cranny in between, if you know what I mean.

'Nice to meet ya…' Meeting Mike Munro moments after the surprise. You can tell he's both proud and intimidated to meet me.

So there I was, lying facedown on the soft velvet table. I had not a stitch on. I closed my eyes and waited with mounting excitement for the warm, scented oil to be applied to my skin by the caring hands of one of the beautiful, scantily clad physical therapists. The anticipation of what was soon going to happen triggered a flow of blood through my body that had an immediate effect on key areas of my anatomy. I held my breath and waited – and waited . . . and waited . . .

Ah, at last I felt fingers. But these were not soft, caressing digits, they were cold, stumpy and bony, and they were poking me roughly in the back. 'A little lower, darling,' I said, thinking to myself that I'd been stuck with a rookie.

Suddenly a voice boomed, 'Reg Reagan?'

I spun around on the table, expecting to see a beautiful masseuse wearing high heels and nothing else. But I got the shock of my life as a pasty-faced bloke with a smirk from ear to ear announced: 'Reg Reagan! This is your life!'

I'll be buggered if it wasn't bloody Mike Munro and his TV crew. I could have killed him. 'F**k off!' I roared, furious that he'd interrupted my treatment.

Munro continued, 'Reg, back at the studio we have hundreds of your closest family and friends, and they're waiting to celebrate your life in front of a national TV audience of millions!' He'd backed me into a corner. I reluctantly climbed off the velvet table, pulled on my strides and headed to Channel Nine for a trip down memory lane.

When I arrived on the set the audience applauded me wildly. I looked out into the throng and saw the beaming faces of so many of my old acquaintances. There was John Laws. David Beckham and Sir Alex Ferguson were sitting with Bono from U2. Robert De Niro and Arnold Schwarzenegger were in the third row. And wasn't that Tommy Raudonikis and Roy Masters on either side of Oprah Winfrey? They were all there . . . Mark Taylor and Cathy Freeman, Shane Dye and Gorden Tallis. All my brothers and sisters and my mum. My old man, Ray Reagan, looked pissed off and proud all at the same time. And, of course, there in the very front row of the vast auditorium was my wife, Ruth, and our kids, Reg Jnr, Randy and Rick.

Looking around, I saw old mates, girlfriends and lovers. The joint was packed. My head spun as each familiar smile I saw triggered recollections. 'Isn't *this* going to be a shitfight!' I thought standing on the stage, my smile as fake as my Rolex watch.

Then Munro strode through the curtains. He told me to take a seat and strap myself in while he invited all these people from my past to come up and share with the nation their memories of the events that shaped my life. But after about 20 minutes, I was starting to get pissed off with sitting there listening to these wankers I hardly knew carving me up in front of millions.

Just as Mike Munro called Andrew Johns and Gorden Tallis onto the stage, I decided I'd had enough. 'That'll do!' I hollered. 'That will f**kin' do! Fair dinkum, Munro, first you drag me here kicking and screaming from my physiotherapy session, and now I have to listen to others trying to tell me how great my life has been! I *know* how great it's been. Look! If you bludgers want this show to continue, then everybody sit down and shut up, people at home go and grab a cuppa, take a piss and get ready for the best two hours of your life as Reg Reagan delivers his *own* story!'

Sprung!

As Channel Nine went to a commercial break, producers rushed around finding new timeslots for regular programs and axing some altogether to make way for this piece of television history. The nation held its breath and Nine's ratings rocketed as word spread that the warts-and-all version of the life of Australia's favourite son and mightiest hero, as told by the great man himself, was about to be screened. The director called out, 'Back on air in 15 seconds.'

All of what you're about to read is as real as my moustache, so I refused Mike Munro's demand that I submit to a lie detector test, and prepared to bare my soul. My life had been colourful and controversial, and I promised myself not to tone it down one bit, no matter what deep shit my confessions landed me in. This is my story . . .

2
THE MAKING OF ME

M+Y GRANDFATHER, Rene, was a Parisian taxi driver. He *owned* the narrow, winding streets of Montparnasse and Saint-Germain. Like his illustrious grandson, Rene was hugely respected by all, but, unlike yours truly, he was not well liked. He had a short fuse and his patience level was zero. He drank rough plonk for breakfast and had horrendous BO. I suppose you could say he was a typical Frenchman.

Grandma Roni was a Dutch wharfie, whose heavily tattooed arms slung containers around the rough docks of Oosterbeek and Zandvoort. She was streetwise, tough and, thanks to a diet of raw herrings, stronger than most men. At the same time, Gran was a warm and loving woman, and in her youth she was known as the most passionate kisser in all the Netherlands.

It was in the year of 1925 they met and fell in love on a Contiki tour of Italy, Greece and Bratislava. There were no

'It's a boy!' Young Reggie at six months old. I've got my dad's eyes and my grandma's mo.

streamlined buses then, of course, the tourists travelled by horse and buggy, but just like today they got paralytic drunk and spewed on local religious icons and art treasures. Granddad and Grandma were in their element and, in his words, they screwed their way across Europe.

Imagine their shock when Granddad introduced her to his mum and dad and they labelled her a slut. Well, as you'd expect, Pop got mighty pissed off at that and told them to go and jam it up their saggy old arses. All in French, of course.

That sad and fateful night, Rene asked Roni for her hand, the one with 'Death Or Glory' tattooed on it. She thought about his marriage proposal for a while, then suggested to Pop that to really make sure they were ready, they should go on *Blind Date*. Pop hated shows like that and told Gran it was now or never. She finally said, 'Yes!' – or '*Oui!*'

Just like today, buying a flat or duplex in Paris or Amsterdam was very expensive. The newlyweds decided they should start their life together somewhere new, where people would accept their unconventional love, and their kids to come could have a backyard to play in.

My grandparents put all their belongings in a suitcase, hopped on the first steamer to the South Seas . . . and disembarked in New Guinea. Unfortunately, life among the coconut trees and cannibals was too much of a culture shock – and Gran really hated it. So, they caught the first boat to Sydney.

Granddad and Grandma loved the Land Down Under from the start, the climate and beaches, the tolerant, good-natured locals. Sure, people called them 'bloody wog' and 'stupid dago' all the time, but usually with a smile on their face. Good old Aussie humour is nothing new.

Soon they had the first of their seven children: my father, Ray. Dad grew up in a loving home in the western suburb of Homebush, then famous only for its abattoir and shark attacks in the local bay every other week. Ray was a typical Aussie kid. He attended school, played sport and loved banging sheilas. His slight French accent and dark Mediterranean looks made him a smash hit with the lady folk.

He played the field for 10 years or so. Then, when he was 17, he met the girl of his dreams at a blue light disco. She was short, stocky and had personality-plus. Her name was Rose Smith. They dated, but, like all young lovers, had their ups and downs. Not the least of their issues was my father's trouble keeping his dick in his pants. On Dad's 21st birthday, after skolling his yard glass and being violently sick over the family dog, Rex, he finally asked Mum to marry him.

Dad was a natural showman and popped the question in front of all his family and friends. There wasn't a dry eye in the house, mainly due to the fact that these so-called friends were screwing Rose behind Dad's back. But for all his faults, Dad was a forgiving man in those days. Let bygones be bygones, was his motto. And so began the life together of Ray and Rose Reagan.

Dad wasted no time in the nookie stakes and soon Rose was spitting out kids. First came my sister, Regan Reagan; then Ray Jnr. Regan and Ray were such pricks of kids that Dad wanted to have a vasectomy. But, as a good Catholic, Mum insisted it was morally wrong and in the future they used condoms.

Mum and Dad loved the drive-in, and every Saturday night the old man would take the Sandman for a spin and they'd catch a flick. Once they went to watch a film Mum reckoned deserved an R rating at least. By intermission, Ol' Rose was desperate for a Drumstick and Ray was keen to dive into some fairy floss. Like randy cats they banged away, and at the penultimate moment the rubber broke. I was only nine months off.

Mum reckons it was the labour from hell, but after 72 hours I got bored. To the relief of all, I emerged into the big, wide world. A legend was born, and Mum and Dad had their most beautiful and talented child.

At 2 stone 1 ounce, it was fair to say I was a healthy baby, and the doc – as well as the editors of the *Guinness Book of Records* – was amazed at my thick black body hair. Reporters from the *Sydney Morning Herald* got wind of my birth and came to take photos for their weekly 'Believe It Or Not' feature. Mum kept the clipping, headed: 'Is Baby Reg the Missing Link? Fat, hairy child may hold key to Theory of Evolution.'

Naturally, Mum and Dad were proud as punch and took me home to their modest bungalow in Homebush a few days later. All the neighbourhood came to my cot to gaze in wonder. Somehow they knew I was special, that a child had been born who would grow up to inspire millions.

3

THE REAGAN BUNCH

WHILE I WAS A TODDLER, Dad was doing it tough. After they closed down the Homebush abattoir, work was scarce for stun-gun operators in the western suburbs of Sydney. So, he and Mum moved us all to the coalfields of Cessnock, up Newcastle way, where he found work in the mines.

My first recollections are of playing in the backyard, aged three, with Regan and Ray Jnr and my dog, Rafael, who was named after my great-grandfather back in France. He was dead by then, of course. Sadly, Dad's faithful dog, Rex, was no longer with us either. He was eaten by a grey nurse shark while retrieving a stick Ray Jnr threw into Homebush Bay.

I'd be lying if didn't say I was a wonderful child. I was so good, in fact, that my parents' faith in children was restored, and in rapid succession out popped Rhonda, Roslyn, Ryan, Rick and Ron, the last named after my great-uncle, a fading

'… and the cat's in the cradle …' Ray Reagan leaving the family home, on his way to the brothel. I'm checking his coat pocket for rubbers!

Hollywood movie star who'd told us in his last Christmas card that he'd like to have a shot at politics one day.

I had a golden childhood but had to put up with my share of teasing. On my first day at Cessnock primary, some Year 6 kids decided to give it to me about my moustache. Luckily, I was a big bastard and Dad had made me take boxing lessons, so I was able to punch seven shades of shit out of the lot of 'em. My pugilistic skills came in very handy as I grew up. Whether it was a smartarse schoolmate or a big-noting deputy principal, they all got a short, sharp lesson in why it was wise to give young Reggie Reagan the respect he deserved.

Although I was a hardnut, I was also a mummy's boy. Some people thought it was wrong that I was still breastfeeding at 10. A few even thought it was kinky. I didn't care. All I knew was that I adored the old girl dearly and loved the taste of breast milk on my Coco Pops each morning.

Around that time I really began to get into sport. I was a Golden Gloves boxer, a state cricket rep and captain–coach of the under-11 regional Rugby League side. I was earmarked as a future star in a multitude of sports, and while such praise can go to a young 'un's head, my family, friends, minders and publicist kept me grounded.

I also had a wonderful sense of humour. As my mum wrote in her diary: *Every Friday morning, a group of nuns from the Catholic Bridge Club and I would go off for a bushwalk, just to try to keep the weight off. Well, on more than one occasion, Reg disguised himself in a hat and trench coat, and jumped out from behind a tree and exposed himself to us all. All the other women screamed in terror, but I just pissed myself laughing. The sight of Reg's little willy flying in the breeze was* so cute. Actually, I shouldn't say 'little willy', because my boy's penis was probably larger than a fully grown Asian man's, even then.

The nuns weren't the only ones I played tricks on. Cessnock summers were pretty hot and we didn't have a backyard pool, so all the Reagan kids spent our Christmas holidays at the local Olympic Baths. When my older brother, Ray Jnr, went back to school at the end of January, his teacher asked him to write an essay on 'The Most Interesting Thing That Happened in the Holidays'. Here's what he wrote:

One f**kin' scorcher of a day when the pool was jam-packed, Reggie and his little brother, Ron, decided to get up to a bit of mischief. Reg told Ron he was going to do the time-honoured Reagan fake-poo trick. He sent Ron to the kiosk to buy a Chokito bar, then he made him unwrap it, hop in the pool, and let the Chokito float around. Then he had to climb out and yell, 'My God! There's a King Henry in the water!' The swimmers would be totally f**kin' freaked out and leave the pool quick-smart. That was the cue for Ron to dive in, swim up to the chocolate bar, which everyone thought was a piece of crap, and eat it. Well, off they went, and I tell ya, it worked a f**kin' treat!!! Everyone was screaming and yelling hysterically. Then Reg gave Ron the wink. It was our little bro's turn to deliver the big punchline. So Ron dives in and the f**kin' little show pony butterflies over to the chocolate bar. The crowd was bellowing in horror. Without hesitating, Ron picks up the Chokito and swallows it in one go. Only problem was that Reggie had doublecrossed him and it was a real turd. Ron screamed and fainted. He sank to the bottom of the

pool and had to be rescued by a lifeguard. The poor bastard nearly died because no one would give him mouth-to-mouth. Happily, after he got over his hepatitis, Ronny was able to see the funny side. That was the most interesting thing that happened in my summer holiday.
(signed) Ray Reagan Jnr.

The teacher gave Ray 2.5 out of 20 for the essay, one of the highest marks he ever got in his school career.

Through my teens, my early sporting ability proved no flash in the pan. The older I got, the better I got. You name the sport, I played it and played it bloody well. Basketball, Rugby League, athletics, cricket, swimming, boxing; I was a natural at every one.

The only cloud on my horizon was when Mum got retrenched from her job as a checkout chick at the supermarket, and the old man had to do what his own father had done in the streets of Paris and drive a cab at nights to make ends meet. Dad loved work. As well as digging coal and hooning around in his taxi, he laid bricks at the weekend to unwind. With Dad occupied 24/7, I had no one to drive me all over town to my many sporting events. So I was told to pick one and piss the rest off.

The choice was easy. Rugby League was my first sporting love. I was only 15, but knew I had a huge future in the game. I could play any position brilliantly, of course, but found a home at lock-forward, and amazed the junior coaches with my mix of skill, athleticism and the kind of raw aggression that can only be described as hate-motivated violence. I threw myself into training and put on size and muscle. I spent hours down at the park developing my ball skills and footwork.

THIS IS MY LIFE!

Modesty aside, I was way too good for the other 15-year-olds, so my coach, Digger Tomlinson, recommended I step up and play for the Cessnock under-18s. Their coach was a bloke named Wacka Williams. At first Wacka thought I wouldn't handle the big jump. He reckoned that I'd be belted and intimidated by the older, bigger kids. But he agreed to take me on and see how I went.

Before my first game I was pretty nervous, especially as our opponents, Maitland, hadn't been beaten for 15 months and were a huge and nasty side who loved inflicting punishment on their rivals. Teams coming up against Maitland got so shit-scared they were beaten before they ran onto the paddock.

After the pre-game warm-up, we were sitting in the sheds waiting for Wacka and our captain, Mick Sheridan, to give us our final instructions. Wacka spoke briefly about not being overawed and told us to get out there and try to do our best. I thought his speech was pretty pissweak. Then it was our fearless leader's turn and, let me tell you, Mick was shitting himself deluxe. He was shaking and stuttering so much he could barely get the words out. I looked around at the other boys and they also wore looks of terror.

I stood up and gave it to Mick: 'Piss off home, you f**king shirt-lifter! I can't stand the sight of you!'

Wacka tried to restore order. 'Now, Reg, please, some respect . . .'

I cut him off. 'You piss off too! You couldn't coach a bear to shit in the forest! Boys, from this moment, follow my lead!'

It's time now for me to own up to something else that some of you may be surprised to know. I have a vicious and violent side to my personality, and that afternoon I surpassed myself. For the next 80 minutes I tore into those Maitland blokes with unbridled fury. I did anything and everything to get an advantage. I grabbed genitals. I used my elbows, knees and fingers to cause maximum damage to my opponents. Once I even used the linesman's flag to perform what could only be described as a colonoscopy on my opposite number. The crowd swelled as word passed around the district that Ray Reagan's boy was wreaking havoc at the Cessnock Showground.

To cut a long story short, we won. I scored the winning try and even shagged a few of the Maitland cheerleaders around the back of the grandstand after the match.

Next day I got a phone call from Bluey Bailey, who coached the Cessnock Goannas first grade team. He asked me to play for him the following week, saying he'd been gob-smacked by my game against the Maitland under-18s. He'd thought I was a mental case the way I ripped in and tore my opponents apart. 'Thanks, Bluey,' I replied. 'But why don't you stick your precious first grade team up your wrinkly old arse.' I then hung up on him. It was only after I discovered the Goannas put on free piss after the match that I reconsidered. I rang Bailey back. 'Bluey,' I said, 'I'm your man!'

I lapped up the whole first grade experience. It was an opportunity to really test myself against quality opponents week in, week out. My teammates took me under their wing and I loved the social side.

I was only a kid, but the local pub became my second home. I began dating older women, and this was a wonderful experience. Let me tell you, I was the only 15-year-old with a 48-year-old girlfriend. Her name was Helen. When

I took her to the school dance, my school pals really put me on a pedestal.

We finished the season in fourth place and I was named the comp's Rookie of the Year. I was rapt to receive the award and slept with the trophy that night . . . as soon as I sent Helen back home to the retirement village.

Bluey Bailey was a good mate of Roy Masters, who was then coach of Sydney's Western Suburbs Magpies and is now a renowned sportswriter. Unbeknown to me, Bluey had tipped Roy off that I was someone the famous Black and Whites should sign before the other Sydney clubs got wind of my mighty talent. Roy secretly turned up to a few of our games and liked what he saw.

One night I was at the pub drinking piss, womanising, and otherwise preparing for my School Certificate, when the phone rang. The barmaid handed it to me. It was Roy. He wanted me to come to Sydney the next day for a yarn about maybe joining the Magpies. I didn't hesitate. Wests were my kind of team. They were a bunch of rough-and-ready brawlers infamous for their violent play – especially against their hated rivals, the flash and cashed-up Manly–Warringah Sea Eagles – and the long suspensions handed out to their stars every week. But they could play footy too, and were among Sydney's top three teams. I went straight home and talked the old man into taking a day off from the mine and driving me to Sydney. Then I went straight to bed and had sweet dreams of ol' Reggie Reagan spreading some Sydney prick's nose all over his face in the Big League.

4
REG REAGAN, BOY WONDER

I AWOKE THE MORNING of my meeting with Roy Masters in a state of wild excitement. I was dead keen to make the right impression on the formidable coach. My old man, as usual, gave me his advice. 'Son,' he said, and I could have sworn the emotion of the moment was making this tough old bugger get all teary, 'whenever Mr Masters talks to you, look him straight in the eye, he'll respect that. And in the meeting be sure to pass some disparaging remarks about homosexuals and coloured people. This'll show him you're a real man.' I appreciated Dad's good intentions. However, this statement made me realise what a f**kin' out of touch social dinosaur he'd become.

My uncle Ralph volunteered to drive Dad and me down to Sydney, so we bought a couple of cartons of KB to settle our nerves on the long ride.

Posing with the U/9s. By the way, that's me middle row, dead centre.

The drive was a hoot. We picked up three Swedish backpackers hitchhiking at Gosford – top birds, too. Dad, Ralph and I entertained the sheilas by singing Dr Hook songs, until Ralph, who'd not been this close to a good sort in 40 years, suffered a near-nervous breakdown in the middle of 'Sylvia's Mother'. There may have been another reason for Uncle Ralph's seizure. At Hornsby, Dad got lucky, and the sight of your brother getting a blow-job can trigger some strange emotions.

By the time we dropped the sheilas off in Bondi and arrived at Lidcombe Oval, home ground of the Magpies, Dad and I were tanked. Ralph took off. He said he had some pressing business with his accountant in Kings Cross and he'd be back in a couple of hours to pick us up.

Walking across Lidcombe's hallowed turf on my way to Wests' administration offices, I was overcome with awe. Right there, in the middle of the ground, I closed my eyes and imagined scoring the winning try in a big game. I started chanting, 'Rea*gan*, cha, cha, cha! Rea*gan*, cha, cha, cha!' I was in a trance until the sound of Dad spewing nearby snapped me out of it.

Masters met Dad and me and led us inside his office. He wrote about the momentous meeting in his best-selling memoir *Fibro and Face-slapping*:

> *When you are told you are meeting a 15-year-old hopeful you expect to see a fresh-faced kid still in school uniform and shy as all hell. But I couldn't tell young Reg Reagan and his father apart. They both sported wild facial hair and stank of piss. I didn't think much of Ray. At first he wanted to fight me and then every five minutes he*

challenged me to an arm wrestle. All through the meeting Ray kept falling asleep and mumbling about not trusting gays or wogs. Eventually I had to remove him from my office while Reg and I came to terms. I signed Reg up on the spot because I knew he'd fit right in at Wests. The kid had so much hate in him it was running out of his ears, and this suited our aggressive attitude. Deal done, Reg and I shook hands and emerged from the office into the corridor outside. Imagine my shock when I found Ray Reagan having oral sex with my secretary's statue of Buddha.

Masters told me that Sydney football was a lot different from the league I played in the bush. He told me to go home and pack my gear, and be in Sydney within a month so he could get me into shape for the start of the season. Back in Cessnock I got stuck into training. I lifted weights, I ran up steep hills, I shagged sheilas.

Roy had drummed into me that if I was going to make it in first grade I'd have to be prepared to make sacrifices. I showed him how serious I was by having one night off the piss every single week. Yep, every Monday evening I gave the KB the flick, and instead went over to Uncle Ralph's joint and had a Fijian night when we wore grass skirts and drank shitloads of kava.

By the time I was on the train to Sydney a few weeks later I was in awesome shape. I resembled Lee Majors. I had muscles on my muscles, and when Roy met me at Lidcombe station he was mighty pleased with the way I looked.

I understood that because I was still a boy, the coach would billet me at his house until I found my feet in the big smoke. But Roy had a great idea. He said it would be better for my blooding as a Magpie if I moved in with a couple of the senior Wests players. Roy said the two blokes he had in mind were seasoned first graders and sure to set me a good example. That sounded OK by me. I didn't know any of my new teammates, but figured footballers are footballers wherever you go.

Tommy Raudonikis and Les Boyd met me at the door of their home unit. From somewhere in the joint came a weird smell, like someone had marinated dogshit then deep-fried it. The TV was tuned to *The Great Temptation*, Led Zeppelin were blasting out riffs on the stereo, ashtrays and empty beer cans occupied every flat surface, and there was congealed blood all over the green shagpile carpet.

Tommy and Les had lots in common, country boys who'd represented their country in Rugby League. Yet, they were in some ways different. Tommy had the gift of the gab. He could sit and talk to a total stranger for hours before he punched his head in. Les was very quiet and not as articulate as Tommy. He preferred to knock someone out right after shaking hands.

Gee, those blokes were good to me. Every night they took me to a pub on Parramatta Road, where we got legless. They were deeply impressed by how much piss a 15-year-old could put away.

With my dad, Ray, back in Cessnock, Tommy and Les became father figures to me. They held the bucket when I barfed and were always passing on valuable advice. When the club enrolled me at St Gregory's high school at Campbelltown, they pulled me aside to say school was for morons, and reading and writing were for soft cocks.

A good tip, I reckoned, so, just like them, I became a full-time professional footballer.

THIS IS MY LIFE!

I tell you, those Wests boys were a real tough, no-nonsense bunch... Les and Tommy, big Dallas Donnelly, Bob Cooper... Not only were they fine players but they all had a great sense of humour. Like at my very first training session. At the Magpies there's a fine old tradition that began in the days of Noel Kelly and Peter Dimond. At the start of each season all the new blokes get bashed up, held down, and their eyebrows, legs and pubic hair are shaved clean. When my turn came I didn't put up a fight. The rest of the boys gathered around as Bobby Cooper and Dallas Donnelly took a Bic disposable razor to my eyebrows and legs, and whipped off my shorts and jocks. But the joke was on them. I was only 15 and didn't have a pube to save myself. 'What are you going to do now, ya smartarses,' I crowed.

Dallas showed me. He poured petrol on my genitals and set fire to my prick. I have to admit, even I laughed as I looked down at the roaring blaze.

It hurt like hell, and I still have the scars. But in retrospect, there was one good thing to come of my fiery initiation. My dick is black to this day, and the sheilas at the RSL love it.

5

PECKING ORDER

All through the summer months, I trained with the Magpie first graders, drank with them, fought back to back with them, got thrown into jail with them. But coach Roy Masters still saw fit to start me in the under-23s. I told him he had absolute shit for brains for treating me so shoddily. I was only 15, yes, but I was big, mean, and sported more facial fuzz than any of the older blokes. Roy backed down a bit when I threatened to rip his head off and eat it, and replied that if I proved myself in the lower grade he'd consider me for the firsts, despite my age.

In the early games I struggled – by my own high standards, that is. Sure, I was scoring two or three tries every game and topping the tackle count, but I was only up against 22-year-olds. I had a heart-to-heart with a few of the older first graders and they said that, despite my great talent,

'And how's the family…?' Re-acquainting myself with an opposition player just moments before kickoff.

Pecking Order

playing against experienced hardheads in the top grade at this early stage of my career would be just too big an ask. They ate kids like me for breakfast.

I appreciated my fellow Magpies' concern for my safety – but f**k 'em – first grade was where I wanted to be. I upped my training and vowed to make it impossible for Masters not to pick me. I set a deadline of mid-season to get the big call-up.

One night after training I arrived home to a surprise. Tommy and Les had put on a 16th birthday party for me. I was really touched. All the players and coaching staff were there, crammed into our little home unit with the green carpet. The boys turned on a stripper and filled me full of piss. So full of piss, in fact, that I had to be rushed to St Vincent's Hospital to have my stomach pumped.

I awoke next morning in the emergency ward with a drip in each arm and a thermometer up my arse. The doctor wanted to keep me under his care for a few days, but I had a game to play that afternoon and I couldn't let the boys down. So I checked myself out and hitchhiked to Belmore Oval, where I tore Canterbury to shreds in my best game since coming to Sydney. I felt like shit, but somehow I was able to score three tries and set up two.

The next week at Lidcombe Oval, against Parramatta, I put in another brilliant performance in the under-23s and got myself half a game in reserve grade. When I belted the shit out of a couple of has-beens and crossed for the winning try after an 85-metre run, Roy Masters took note. He wasn't the only one. Reported the *Daily Mirror*'s league scribe the following day:

> *I arrived at Lidcombe Oval early, just in time to watch the under-23s, and I was treated to a performance by*

THIS IS MY LIFE!

16-year-old Reg Reagan that stamped him as a future superstar of Rugby League. Reagan has it all: clever ball-playing; power running; and terrifying aggression, which led to a number of cautions for punching, biting, kicking, hair-pulling, eye-gouging, elbowing, frequent use of the squirrel grip, and foul language heard all over the ground. 'Poofter!' 'Arsewipe!' 'Shitkicker' and 'F—wit!' were some of his milder expletives.

The *Mirror* reporter continued:

The young Reagan left the field to a standing ovation from the Magpie faithful, who waved their editions of Collins English Dictionary X-rated Edition. *But the best was yet to come. Reagan was thrown into the reserve grade game when the result was in the balance. Immediately, he swung the game Wests' way. In a 20-minute period he dominated his older rivals and rounded off his venomous display by crossing for the match-winning try, which spawned a try-scoring celebration that the 20,000 Westies present will never forget. After planting the ball between the posts, he stripped naked and took off on a length of the field dash. The Magpie faithful went beserk as Reagan's long hair and even longer penis flew dangerously in the breeze. At the end of his 100m burst, in which he was timed at 10.05 (a new Australian record), he scaled the goalpost, sat on the crossbar, and remained until the final siren seven minutes later. This unassuming and level-headed young superstar-to-be left the field to his second standing ovation of the afternoon. This time the fans waved frankfurts in the air to show their devotion to a young man who is surely our game's next pin-up boy.*

One thing about me is that I don't get carried away with media hoopla. I knew I was flavour of the month, but I also knew how fickle stardom can be. I was determined to remain as humble as possible under the circumstances. But who could blame me for pinning the *Mirror* article up on the players' noticeboard? After all, it *was* accurate. I was better than any of my under-23 teammates. I also reckoned it would put pressure on Masters to pick me for the top team.

My ploy worked a treat. After training that night, Roy came up to me and shook my hand. 'Congratulations, Reg. You've been selected in first grade.'

Tommy and Les weren't about to let such a career milestone pass without a party, so they took me to the pub to celebrate. What a night. I called Mum and Dad from the bar to tell them I'd made first grade. Mum shed a tear and told me how proud she was. Dad shed a tear and told me he had crabs.

Next night at training I was made fully aware of the enormity of being named a first grader. Not only was I the youngest player ever to play top grade Rugby League in the Sydney Premiership, but the next match was against our most hated rivals, Manly–Warringah. It was class warfare between our clubs. We were the Fibros, battlers from Sydney's west, who made do with local talent because we couldn't afford imports. They were the Silvertails, highly-paid glamour boys from the glitzy northern beaches, mercenaries plundered from struggling clubs by a cashed-up Sea Eagles management. Whenever Wests and Manly clashed, it was guaranteed bloody mayhem.

The night before the match I was so excited I couldn't sleep. I tried everything to make me nod off: alcohol, nicotine, masturbation. Nothing worked.

THIS IS MY LIFE!

So I climbed out of my cosy fold-up bed in the laundry of our unit and watched a bit of TV. There was a documentary about Muhammad Ali on, and it fired me up even more. I eventually dozed off around 3 am, until awoken at 8 am by Tom Raudonikis squatting on my face and performing a follow-through fart.

When I got to Lidcombe Oval, there were heaps of supporters there wearing the black and white of Wests. Some, as I signed their autograph books, gave me valuable snippets of advice, like 'Kill those Sea Eagle bastards!'

Thirty minutes before kickoff we were all getting our footy gear on in the sheds. I was between John Dorahy and Graeme O'Grady, and they were wising me up: 'Don't run at Terry Randall,' and 'Watch Johnny Gibbs's sidestep.' To be honest, their advice was going in one ear and out the other, I was so focused on the size of some of my teammates' penises.

Nine minutes before kickoff, Roy called us into the middle of the room. He'd come up with an ingenious plan. Instead of starting slowly and working our way into the game, he wanted us to start right from the kickoff with fire blazing out of our arses and blow Manly off the park. To get us in the necessary homicidal frame of mind, Roy ordered us to slap the Christ out of each other before we ran on, and then, when we were all foaming at the mouth and our eyes were spinning like pinwheels, we'd give it to the Sea Eagles good and proper. 'OK, boys, grab a partner and friggin' rip into each other!' yelled Roy.

Everywhere I looked, my teammates were slapping each other's faces. Tommy had Bob Cooper bleeding. Dallas Donnelly was giving 'Joe Cool' Dorahy an awful hiding. Fair dinkum, it was as if I'd died and gone to heaven. Problem was, I couldn't find a partner on whom I could unleash the fire and hate I had in my belly. So I grabbed the sandboy and gave the little prick the belting of his life. By the time Roy dragged me off that seven-year-old kid he looked like roadkill. We sprinted onto Lidcombe Oval ready for war.

The first half went by in a flash. Manly kicked off and the ball went straight to Tommy Raudonikis. He hurled it straight back over his head and just started throwing punches. There was very little football played, just full-on bashing. The crowd went berserk as the teams left the field at half-time with Manly ahead 8–5.

Roy pulled me aside and told me I was getting too caught up in the fighting and forgetting about football. He ordered me to get all the viciousness out of my system right then and there. So I did. Sitting in his wheelchair just to my left was 94-year-old life member Snowy Graves. I spun around and gave Snow a generous tickle-up. When I returned to my senses I apologised to the club legend. Wiping the blood from his mouth, he said he f**king loved it and ordered me to go back out and kill the motherf**kers.

My man of the match performance was hailed as 'a perfect blend of skill, power and thuggery'. Everything I touched in that second half turned to gold, except, of course, Johnny Gibbs's testicles. I made break after break and saved try after try with classic cover defence. We won 21–12 and I'd made the perfect first grade debut. Just as I dreamed they would when I had my first day at Wests, the crowd yelled, 'Rea*gan*, Rea*gan*!'

Coming off the field, I was intercepted by 2SM radio broadcaster Frank Hyde, who gave me his award. 'The Levi

Strauss Man of the Match Prize goes to 16-year-old Western Suburbs wunderkind Reg Reagan,' Frank told his listeners. 'Reg, how do you feel at this moment?'

'Frankly, Frank,' I replied, 'I'm pretty f**ked.' I was too tired for niceties.

'Reg, it looked mighty tough out there.'

'Ah . . . shit, yeah, bloody tough, Frank, very f**king tough.'

'Son, you're only a boy. How did you find those big Manly forwards?'

'Well, Frank, Terry Randall at one stage hit me so hard I shit my pants, so I guess you could say it was tough.'

'Reg, your father must be so proud.'

'Yeah, but to be honest he's preoccupied with getting rid of his crabs right now.'

'Oh, so your father's in the seafood business?'

'No, Frank, he can't keep his cock in his pants.'

'Well, Reg,' said the veteran radio man, 'congratulations. Here's a thirty-dollar cheque courtesy of Levi's.'

The rest of the season went enormously well for me. I picked up a few more of Frank's best player awards and at the end I had enough money saved to buy myself a pair of Levi Strauss bell-bottom trousers. No sooner had I forked out my dough, the bastards went out of fashion.

I won plenty more besides, scooping the New South Wales Rugby League's Best Newcomer prize and winning Wests' Rookie of the Year Award. It was a dream season for me. Only two years before I'd been repeating the seventh grade of high school for the second time. Now, here I was an established Rugby League first grader and budding superstar.

6

WIPED OUT

BEING A RUGBY LEAGUE STAR had its advantages. After the bash, barge and biff of the footy months, the six-month off-season was a great opportunity for me to reacquaint myself with family, friends and groupies. But drinking, smoking and shagging could keep me only so fit, and being a multi-skilled elite athlete, it was important to me to make the most of my extraordinary talents in other sports. And ever since I beat Rabbit Bartholomew to win the Mattara Surfabout Festival in Newcastle as an 11-year-old grommet, one of my real passions has been surfing.

I've always been at home in the sea and, over the years, some famous people have sought my advice about riding the waves, with a board and without. I remember the time our late, lamented prime minister Harold Holt called me at home back in December 1967. Harry said he was thinking

Surfing has always been one of my great passions, along with drinking and screwing. This shot was used in a Quiksilver ad.

of having a swim at Cheviot Beach in Victoria, but the surf was pretty turbulent and he wanted to know whether there was a patrolled beach with flags nearby. 'F**kin' flags!' I roared, 'Harry, you great wuss, be a man and back yourself.'

It's not easy to describe the unique feeling surfing gives me. Being at one with Mother Nature and knowing her awesome power is truly incredible. For total satisfaction, only killing an animal with a .303 or, perhaps, ferreting, comes close.

Now, I'm not one to big-note, but at one stage, not so many years ago, my prowess on a board was so f**king brilliant that when my football obligations ended for the year I went in search of the Endless Summer on the professional surfing tour. Back then, just like today, being a pro-surfer is more than just catching a few waves, soaking up the sun and sinking beers. There's the travel. I enjoyed that at first, but I found after a while that visiting other countries and experiencing different cultures was starting to give me a philosophical outlook. It actually started to curb my competitive nature, which I didn't enjoy, and I began to settle for second best, particularly in nightclubs.

While I persisted with my travelling lifestyle for a little while longer, I was forced to cut it right back. I was living out of a suitcase (or, more to the point, a shower bag), and I was bordering on a nervous breakdown brought on by sheer exhaustion. I got a serious warning shot in Bali, where I nearly bloody died after I was found facedown in a Kuta gutter suffering from extreme heatstroke. When I came around a few days later, the doctors told me I was suffering from severe delusions brought on by the exhaustion. That explained to all and sundry why in the week leading up to my heatstroke, I was wandering around Bali dressed in denim jeans and a leather jacket and would only answer to the name 'Fonzie'. In many ways, I've never been the same again and to this day I find it difficult to say 'I'm sorry', a side effect from my days as the Milwaukee legend.

I returned home after that and took a month off, just to recharge the batteries. I battered myself on the piss during the break, and felt that knocking around some of my old waterholes with backslappers and fair-weather friends would give me that false confidence surge I dearly needed. That did the trick, all right, and once I got back on my board there was no stopping me.

My amazing streak of wins in major surfing events included the XXXX Classic at Burleigh Heads, and, one of my proudest moments, winning the Rip Curl Pro at Bell's Beach in Victoria.

I was so hot on my stick, you couldn't pick up a newspaper without seeing my face – or bare arse – on the front page. I was unbeatable on Australian beaches. But then mates began pressuring me to get fair dinkum and chase the world title. Trouble was, I now rarely travelled overseas because of doctors' orders to curb my intense schedule, and my basic intense dislike of foreigners. I'd distrusted them ever since I was a kid, when Dad told me that anyone from another country was a shirt-lifter. 'I'm the son of a Frenchman, so I know what I'm talking about,' he'd say. I know now that this is not necessarily true, but old habits die hard and every time I leave Australia my heart bleeds and my arsehole twitches.

But old Reg has never knocked back a challenge and that year I either won or was runner-up at all the events on the Surfing Professionals World Championship Tour. Tahiti's

Teahupoo, Fiji's Cloudbreak, Rio Norte in Brazil, Portugal and France; no beach presented a problem for me. Finally, it came to the make-or-break contest in Hawaii. If I could win the fabled Pipeline Masters at the Banzai Pipeline on Oahu's north shore, I'd take my rightful place as world surfing champion.

At Sydney airport, where I was catching my flight to Honolulu, I was overcome by a tide of goodwill, thanks to three or four thousand close mates who turned up to crack a farewell KB and wish me luck. As I crowd-surfed through customs, held aloft by my admirers, it struck me like a kick up the arse that I wasn't just doing this for myself. No, I was doing it for my army of fans, for the barmen down at my local, and most of all, for the little guys out there who, like me, have big dreams but, unlike me, don't have the talent, dedication and charisma.

On the plane, I overcame my nerves by getting shit-faced. The flight attendant handed me my 30th KB, then told me to tone it down a bit and prepare for takeoff. I followed her orders as my guts rumbled and sweat started pouring down my face. I'm good at most things, but not at flying. This dates back a few years when I was returning from Europe. The copilot had apparently eaten a crook prawn in France and was suffering from a massive dose of food poisoning. Then, wouldn't you know it, the captain starts getting heart palpitations. Basically, without a miracle, we were goners. Luckily for all on board, the miracle was sitting in Economy Row 57 Seat E (the tight pricks wouldn't give me an upgrade!) and from Singapore right through to Sydney, I took control of that jumbo. Apart from a bit of a dodgy landing (I brought the plane down in Pitt Street), it couldn't have been a better flight. Regardless of my heroics, since then flying has spooked me and my policy has always been to get paralytic before takeoff.

My mates had warned me about drinking heavily at altitude, and when I awoke from my stupor as the plane landed at Honolulu, I knew what they were on about. Fair dinkum, I had a monster hangover. My head was pounding like a jackhammer and my mouth tasted like a cat had shat in it. Oddly enough, one had. The old bag sitting next to me was smuggling half a dozen felines into Hawaii in her strides. Five died from the smell, but one moggy escaped and mistook my gob for a kitty litter while I was passed out.

My surfing mates, Matt Hoy and Damien Hardman, were at Honolulu airport to meet me. They hoisted me out of the arrivals lounge and into the back of their car. We were off to the north shore of Hawaii and the treacherous Banzai Pipeline. On the way across the island, as they raced through plantations of pineapples, Hoyo and Dooma told me about the dangers of the Pipeline, how the waves there were huge and even the most experienced surfers had been cut to ribbons when they wiped out on the razor-sharp coral just below the surface. I pretended to listen.

The only thing they said that penetrated my befuddled brain was that in just one hour all the surfers had to attend the Duke Kahanamoku Tribute Ceremony, an annual ritual to honour the legendary Olympic swimmer and boardrider who introduced surfing to Australia, New Zealand and the United States. The Duke died in 1968 but he remains a god to Hawaiians, and the ceremony on the golden sands of Sunset Beach is attended by tens of thousands of surfers and the world's media. The boys said that as *the* hot surfer on the tour, the organisers and the Duke's family were hoping I would get up on stage and say a few words in praise of the great man. 'No problem, fellas, tell 'em it'll be an honour,' I said. Thanks to my Rugby League achievements, I'd been feted at numerous awards ceremonies and figured this wouldn't be too different.

But at Sunset Beach, I looked in awe and disbelief at the huge and passionate crowd that had gathered around the statue of the Duke. Many laid flowers, others wept and prayed. Jesus, I thought, this ain't the Dally Ms. The prospect of making a speech to this bunch made me feel like I was about to shit my pants.

'Quick,' I told Hoyo and Dooma, 'get me some KBs, and make it snappy. Old Reggie Boy has to relax a bit if he's going to pull this off.' All they could scrounge was a carton of Budweiser. The Yank brew tasted like horse piss, but when in Rome . . . and I polished off the lot as the various rituals of reverence took place and my big moment loomed.

Suddenly there was a fanfare of Hawaiian steel guitars and ukeleles, and the master of ceremonies, a direct descendant of the Duke, called me to the stage. The crowd went nuts and strangers draped hibiscus leis around my neck as I pushed through. This was something for them to tell their grandchildren. A living legend had come to honour a dead one.

Now, as a public speaker of vast experience, I know how important it is to get the audience on side from the start, and I always break the ice with a little joke. So when the MC stuck the mike in my face and said, 'Mr Reagan, how much do you know about the Duke?' I pretended to carefully consider my answer for a minute or so. Then I answered, 'I know this much, mate, he's just another dirty Polynesian poofter!'

Unbelievably, no one laughed. In fact, the crowd let out a roar of fury. I tried to defuse their hysteria. 'Shit,' I grinned at one group that was trying to storm onto the stage, 'you lot must have left your sense of humour in your mud huts!'

At that, the MC took a swing at me, and if it wasn't for my perfectly placed kick in his Jatz crackers, who knows what he might have done!

I was about to be torn apart and eaten by angry Hawaiians – I knew how Captain Cook must have felt – when Matty and Damien roared up in their car. I leapt in and we sped off, leaving the mob waving their spears in the distance.

Back in Honolulu I checked into the penthouse suite of the Royal Hawaiian Hotel on Waikiki Beach. Of course, the nosy local media knew I'd be staying at the best pub in town and for the next two hours I fielded call after call from reporters. 'Why the disrespect?' they demanded to know.

I said, 'You don't understand, in Australian, "poofter" means wise and powerful.' Unfortunately, they didn't buy it.

How things had changed. When I arrived in Hawaii, I was a crowd favourite. Now, after all the misunderstandings at the Duke Kahanamoku ceremony, I knew the locals would stop at nothing to keep me from winning the world title. But I had to put their evil bias out of my mind and focus on the job at hand – taming the Pipeline. I figured if I could stay mentally strong, the world title was mine.

Next morning, I blitzed my way through the early heats with pure power surfing. Slowly, the crowd's mood swung from animosity to admiration. There were cheers from the gallery as I did 360s and knee turns, hung five and 10 (at the same time, no mean feat on a 1.5 metre needle-nosed board), cut back, re-entered, and walked up and down the plank like I was strolling to the pub on Saturday morning.

The Hawaiians were warming to my style, but they still weren't getting my humour. After one heat the announcer asked me what I thought of the Pipeline waves. 'They're like Hawaiian men,' I replied, 'totally gutless.' Everyone booed. Some hurled coconuts. Thin-skinned pricks.

I couldn't f**kin' believe it. Here I was, turning on some of my finest surfing, and these ungrateful bastard Hawaiians were trashing me. I had another go at hosing them down. Grabbing the mike, I said: 'Look, everyone, I just want to say I have no hard feelings. I forgive your lack of respect. I really do. I understand that only a generation or two ago you were all living in trees!'

Rapidly re-entering the water, I paddled out for the quarterfinals. My opponents were fellow Aussies Mark Occhilupo and Barton Lynch. Great surfers, but I knew I'd easily beat them, for two very good reasons. I was on fire that day . . . and the night before I'd taken Occy and Barton out on the piss. My confidence was well-placed. Neither one was worth a pinch of shit and I strolled into the semis.

I laughed when I saw my American opponent. 'Well, well, if it's not pretty boy Kelly Slater,' I scoffed. Kelly was seeing Pamela Anderson at the time. Pammy, who's a great gal, was on the rebound from me. We were lovers for a while, and naturally she was dead keen to marry yours truly. I broke her heart when I told her straight, 'Pam, you've got a great set of tits, but you're just too shallow.' She hooked up with Kelly but he was just a fling. Interviewers often ask me if Pam and Kelly's relationship is authentic. 'Oh, yeah,' I say, 'about as real as those rescues she made in *Baywatch*.'

THIS IS MY LIFE!

Slater started well, and I looked to be in trouble. But then, like a blessing from the Big Kahuna, the Pipeline waves, maybe stirred up by an underwater earth tremor on the Kamchatka Peninsula, grew huge and 6-metre sets came pounding in. I was in my element. Extreme life-or-death surfing separates the men from the boys. Kelly wiped out, I stepped up a gear and tore those waves apart. I was in the final the following day.

Now, only one man, Hawaiian Derek Ho, stood between me and the world title, and there was no way I was going to let this grubby looking little suck-arse steal my thunder.

It was the biggest surfing event of my fabulous career, so I thought it wise not to vary my usual pre-final routine. That night I went out and hit the piss big-time in Waikiki, laughing off warnings from other Aussie surfers to watch my back because the locals hated me for the things I'd said about the Duke and would do anything to make me lose.

Honolulu was totally abuzz. In spite of what the guys had told me, everybody I bumped into seemed really friendly and wanted to buy me a drink. Knowing it was against the ancient laws of Hawaii to knock back a free beer, I drank myself silly to avoid offending the natives. And, biggest surprise of all, the most generous guy in the bar was Michael Ho, Derek's brother.

Michael and I chewed the fat for hours but, as the sun started to rise, I decided to have an early night and hit the hay in anticipation of the big final. When I arrived back at my hotel room, you wouldn't believe it – my room had been trashed and, worse, all my boards had been stolen. Dirty Hawaiian pricks – after all I'd done for them.

The situation became hopeless. I couldn't even borrow

a board because fellow surfers feared what the locals would do to them if they helped me. I threw up my arms; what could I do? Then it came to me. Giving up has never been in the Reagan vocabulary, so out I swam in the giant Banzai Pipeline surf, determined to beat their favourite son with a display of body surfing that would make the *real* 'Duke', John Wayne, cheer from his grave in admiration.

I threw myself into it with gusto, but all I got for my trouble was pounding after pounding on the razor-sharp reef. The narrow-minded judges didn't even have the decency to score me. As the siren sounded to end the final, I waded into shore contemplating my surfing future. This was no longer the sport I grew to love watching *Puberty Blues* at the Heddon Greta Drive-In. No, this sport was now dirty to my mind.

As I climbed up to the dais, I decided to do the Australian thing and be humble in defeat. My runner-up speech was brief and to the point. 'Get f**ked! You can stick surfing up your arse. I retire!' And I did.

7
THE PRICE OF GENIUS

JUST BEFORE THE COMMENCEMENT of off-season training, Roy Masters sat me down and told me about the pitfalls of the second year in first grade. So often, young players get carried away, only to be brought back to earth with a thud. Roy had case studies and statistics to prove his point and he told me that it was important for myself, for the Magpies, and for the game of Rugby League, that my enormous potential be realised in the season to come. But I didn't hear a word Roy said. I was still drunk from the night before, and was worried that I'd miss the hair and nail appointment I'd arranged for 4 pm.

You have to see my side of things. I was hardly making a cent out of footy. But my sporting deeds and movie-star looks had made me a hot property on the public-speaking circuit, and with advertisers who were desperate for me to

PLAYBIFF

ENTERTAINMENT FOR WOMEN

Playpooch of the Year

LANG HANCOCK: AUSTRALIA'S SEXIEST MAN

Reg Reagan
CESSNOCK'S OWN
HUNK-A-SPUNK

'How long's a piece of string…?' I was always willing to lend myself to the Arts.

promote their products. There were 16 hair-care companies alone trying to get their mitts on my thick dark locks and flowing moustache. I was not just the new pin-up boy of Rugby League, I was the new pin-up boy of all sport, the David Beckham, Michael Jordan, Jonny Wilkinson of my time.

I was flat-chat starring in TV and radio commercials for shampoos and conditioners, beer, smokes, waterbeds, nudist colonies and Lemon Solo. I was doing what no other footballer before me had been able to do – be a Rugby League tough man *and* a beloved commercial icon.

I told the coaching staff and my teammates that just because I was smoking $200 Cuban cigars, drinking Veuve Clicquot champagne and wearing Armani suits to training, it didn't mean that fame had gone to my head. But it was hard to keep grounded. Even when I went to the corner store to buy a lettuce and a packet of Winnies, I'd find myself hoisted onto the shoulders of strangers and bowed at like some kind of demigod.

In just a year, I'd filled 14 scrapbooks with newspaper stories about me. *Cosmopolitan*'s article was typical of the press I got in those days:

> Man of the Year? There's little doubt that title belongs to young stag Reg Reagan. Whether delivering a cheap shot in back play or sucking on a nicotine stick while riding an untamed colt, it's impossible not to be transfixed by his curvy yet athletic body and brooding good looks. Big companies are lining up to pay him top bucks to sell their products to a new market. On TV, he looks just as comfortable skolling a frosty cold schooner of beer with teammates after training, swinging his luxuriant hair in

slow motion in a shampoo ad, or teaching small children how to blow smoke rings. BRAVO, Señor Reagan!

Bloody heady stuff, you'll agree. Thank God I had Roy, Tommy and Les to make sure I didn't get a swollen head. Whenever they thought I was getting too big for my boots, they'd give me a little sign to let me know they were watching. Like when I came home early from the studio one day and found them playing nude Twister with my girlfriend. I understood at once that they were doing this for my own good. Yep, they were like family.

Roy warned me I'd be a victim of the Tall Poppy Syndrome, and that as my fame grew there'd be jealous people who wanted to cut me down to their size. It didn't take long for TPS to rear its ugly head. Suddenly I found myself under attack from do-gooders who proclaimed it outrageous that a 16-year-old was starring in beer and cigarette commercials. For f**k's sake, get a life! These bastards didn't care who they hauled over the coals. One minute they were having a go at me for swigging KB on camera, the next they were out there trying to ban Asian clothing manufacturers from employing eight-year-olds in sweatshops. Fair dinkum!

But the do-gooders got nowhere with me. I had enormous public support, and anyone could see my condom commercials were done in exquisite taste.

Inevitably, I became a babe magnet. Whenever I went to the pub or a nightclub I was swamped by beautiful women. I did a nude spread for *Playgirl* magazine (again, it was very tasteful), and it fuelled the flames of what was fast becoming the phenomenon known as Reg-mania, or Reagan-mania, depending on which state you lived in. I guess it was like Beatlemania, only much more sexual.

Cleo magazine pleaded with me to enter their 'Bachelor of the Year' competition. For this prestigious meat market they gather notable single men from all over Australia and hold a poll to see which bloke the sheilas would most like to be screwed by. Under my photograph, *Cleo* ran a little 'Reg Reagan Fact File':

> *Full name: Reg Reagan*
> *Likes: Scoring tries, drinking piss and banging birds*
> *Dislikes: Animals (except ferrets)*
> *Favourite TV Show:* Cop Shop
> *Favourite Movie:* Taxi Driver
> *Favourite Actor: Burt Reynolds*
> *Favourite Actress: Linda Lovelace*
> *Sporting Hero: Self, Apollo Creed*
> *If You Won $1 million How Would You Spend It?: Hire a high-class hooker for the day and build a statue of myself*
> *Describe Yourself In Five Words: Handsome, modest, spiteful, great root*
> *Favourite Meal: Lamb chops, chips, a can of KB and a smoke*
> *Pre-Match Meal: The above*
> *Describe Your Ideal Woman: Quiet, weak-natured, big tits, good breeder*
> *Favourite Pastime: Ferreting, shooting, fishing. Anything that involves killing small creatures*
> *Favourite Song: Anything from Sherbet*
> *If You Had 15 Minutes Left To Live, What Would You Do?: Masturbate*

The Price of Genius

Needless to say, I was crowned Bachelor of the Year in a canter. Readers described my honesty as a breath of fresh air, especially when compared to the dumb replies of the other contestants, like Molly Meldrum, Jeff Thomson and Lang Hancock.

I was on a roll: *Cleo* Bachelor of the Year, Rugby League Rookie of the Year, *Ferreting Monthly*'s Man of the Century, and the *Playgirl* centrefold (which I heard was pinned up on women's bedroom walls all over the land, and causing serious issues in the Australian netball and women's cricket team locker rooms).

Then the Tall Poppy Syndrome struck once again, and this time closer to home. My Wests teammates were beginning to turn against me. Unbelievably, they got pissed off when I forgot to turn up at pre-season training. I could see there was serious discontent brewing on one occasion when I had Charles, my driver, drop me off at Lidcombe Oval for a quick chat with the boys before my appearance on *Hey Hey, It's Saturday*. I got the lads in a huddle and gave it to 'em straight. 'Fellas, I know you rely on me, I really do. But what you have to understand is that you're not Robinson Crusoe. All the people of Australia, and many multinational companies, rely on me too.' I then told them what I would have to tell my wife, Ruth, in later years: 'You'll simply have to *share* me!' I pointed out to them that it wasn't *my* fault if beautiful models wanted to have sex with me. It wasn't *my* fault if supporters chanted my name over and over. It wasn't *my* fault that I happened to mention to a reporter from the *Sydney Morning Herald* that I thought my teammates were shit and he plastered my well-meaning quote all over the front page.

As a concession to the boys, I started to come to training

sessions. Not that I ever trained. I compromised. If I had a hairdressing appointment or a nude photo shoot, I simply did it at Lidcombe Oval. As I posed for the cameras, I could see my teammates running 400- and 800-metre fitness sessions. It inconvenienced me, sure, but it was a sacrifice I was happy to make in the interest of team spirit.

Regardless of these little internal rumblings, we started the season well and by round 10 were on top of the ladder. My contribution was, of course, enormous and I was being hailed as a certainty for the representative teams.

Wests were playing great football and having a fine old time off the park as well. It's fair to say the Magpies had a pretty fair drinking culture, and I immersed myself in it. Once, after a big win against St George, we put on a surprise 21st for the likeable halfback Alan Neil. We drank an enormous amount of piss. I passed out, and when I awoke three days later had an incredible hangover. It felt like someone had drilled a hole in my head. Turns out someone f**kin' *had*. Tommy Raudonikis's handiwork with the Black & Decker was definitely a warning that my teammates were consumed by jealousy.

The following week, I turned in another Man of the Match performance against Canterbury, and Channel Seven commentator Rex Mossop that night named me a certain selection in the New South Wales team that would take on the Maroons in Brisbane on the weekend. Now, as usual, I didn't get too carried away. I knew never to count my chickens before they were cooked. After I packed my bags and applied some makeup so I'd look good on the TV news, I went to the pub with my fingers crossed. I sat there with a cold schooner in one hand and a sheila under each arm, ready for the big televised announcement. Suddenly Rex's face was on the pub's TV screen and he was reading out the names of the Blues squad . . . Raudonikis, Boyd, Randall, Goodwin . . . To my absolute horror, mine was not among them.

I had never been so pissed off. Coach Masters tried to settle me down, saying my day would come soon enough. But his comments couldn't calm my anger. And the more I thought about the injustice of my omission, the more furious I became. I was hurting big-time but managed to maintain my dignity when I faced the press. The *Herald* ran 'Reg Says, "My Time Will Come"'. The *Telegraph* headlined 'Reg Says, "Go The Blues"'. The Brisbane *Courier-Mail* exclaimed 'Reg Reagan Labels Selectors Old Cocksuckers'.

My career had been flying along without any hiccups and this was my first real challenge. To be honest, I didn't know how to take it. I just went about doing my usual things: getting pissed every day and spending my nights having sex with beautiful women. Deep down I suppressed my anger and only released it against the opposition on Sundays. Individually I was on fire but the team was starting to struggle. We had dropped to third place and, due to injuries to some key personnel, we were looking scratchy.

Tommy Raudonikis got injured in round 20, and Roy was looking for a captain, someone who could inspire the team like Tommy had. I was deeply honoured, but hardly surprised, when Roy chose me.

We were up against Souths, and I was so proud I got tickets for Mum and Dad to go to Redfern Oval to watch their boy captain the mighty Black and Whites. They arrived at Redfern Oval just in time for the 3 pm kickoff. They had actually got off the train at Redfern station, just up the road from the oval, at midday but were delayed slightly after being mugged and beaten up eight times during the 100-metre walk to the ground.

I was wound up, and my pre-game speech to the boys was a beauty. I won the toss and elected to kick off, a tactic we'd use to intimidate our opponents early on. My final instructions to the boys were: play hard, play tough but play disciplined, and we'll win.

The ref blew game on and Alan Neil kicked off to big Tony Rampling. I flew down the field and hit him with a classic cheap shot. 'Early shower!' said the ref.

Walking off the field, everybody was giving it to me deluxe. The crowd, the Souths blokes, my own teammates, were screaming obscenities. One dirty bastard even spat on me. It was Mum, she hated foul play.

We lost 28–8. I felt I'd let the boys down, but reminded myself I'd been carrying the pricks all year.

The following Tuesday I faced the judiciary. The way they spoke of the incident, it was as if I'd tried to kill the poor bastard. Deep down, I knew that was exactly what I had been trying to do, but wisely kept it to myself. Nonetheless, the judiciary chairman and his band of poo punchers suspended me for six matches. I was devastated. With the semis starting the following week, my season was finished.

Television cameras were shoved in my face straight after the hearing and the emotion spilled over. 'Reg,' one reporter shouted, 'how do you feel?'

'Shithouse. I'm devastated.'

'Reg, what did the chairman say during the hearing?'

'Well, he suspended me for six weeks, unless, of course,

I gave him a blow job. He said if I did, he'd reduce it to two.'

These were comments I came to regret. The upside was that Wests appealed the decision and on my return to the judiciary rooms the chairman reduced my suspension to a fortnight. Who said my days in the Boy Scouts wouldn't come in handy.

It all came to nothing, though. My beloved Magpies, without my talent and expertise, were eliminated in the first week of the finals. It had been a season that taught me so much. Not least, how to handle myself at the judiciary.

8
CAPTAIN AMERICA

ALTHOUGH OUR SEASON didn't finish the way we'd have liked, we were all in pretty good spirits come the end. Again, we'd made the finals and defied critics who claimed we were nothing but a rabble of thugs, alcoholics and no-hopers. I reckoned 'no-hopers' was a bit rough.

We had our usual Mad Monday celebration and booze-up that seemed to go on for days (when, in fact, it went for weeks) and after that we met most nights for a few cold ones. Coach Masters wanted to reward us for a good season and struck a deal with the club that they would go halves with us in forking out for an end-of-season trip.

With tremendous enthusiasm the boys raised the money. We held gambling nights, talent quests and porn and prawn evenings. When we added those funds to the cash some of the boys were able to come up with through blackmail,

Acting as bodyguard for Ronald Reagan moments before he is shot. I was later accused of being pissed. I couldn't see what the problem was.

petty theft and muggings, we were set for the trip of a lifetime.

Roy pulled us together for a meeting to decide where we should go. We all took a vote and narrowed the options down to four destinations. The Philippines, New York, Hawaii or Parramatta. We argued for hours but eventually decided on New York. What swung the vote was the lure of a cruise to the Big Apple before our week there. Yes, the Philippines and Parramatta offered cheap sex, but the prospect of 10 nights on board the *Sea Princess* was too good to resist.

As the luxury cruise liner sailed out of Circular Quay, Tommy and Les celebrated leaving the harbour city by throwing a passenger and a poker machine overboard.

We couldn't believe the *Sea Princess*. Four nightclubs, 22 bars, 32 smoke machines, a casino, a cinema, a concert hall and a wide range of sporting facilities, including six swimming pools. The cruise price was all-inclusive, so we ate and drank everything in sight. We were, as Ricky Martin would say years later, 'Livin' La Vida Loca'. Every day we soaked up the sun and the beer, and got seasick. Word spread quickly that there were champion athletes on board, and it wasn't unusual for a crowd to gather around and watch us drink ourselves stupid in the pool.

We spent our nights in the ship's glamorous nightclubs, where I was king thanks to my incredible dance moves. Fair dinkum, my endurance was phenomenal. It was nothing for me to jive, strut and jitterbug my way through a whole set of 'Stars on 45'. I was so enthusiastic, by the end of the evening the air was filled with the sweet smell of stale beer and ol' Reggie boy's BO. One particular night I was so drenched the boys thought someone had pissed on me. I learned later that this was exactly what had happened. Smartarse Dallas Donnelly relieved himself on yours truly from the club's upper deck.

As I hung my body shirt and flares on the ship's railing to dry out, I made a mental note: The boys are trying to bring you down a peg, Reggie Boy.

By the time we reached New York City we'd worn out our welcome on the *Sea Princess*. To be fair, there were only so many times the skipper could turn a blind eye to our nude sunbaking, using the pokies for shithouses and hurling old ladies overboard.

Once off the Good Ship Lollipop we split up into fours and jumped into yellow cabs. I told our driver: 'The five-star Hilton Hotel, Leroy. And step on the gas!' Sitting there in the back of the taxi as we made our way uptown, I was blown away by the violence and crime I saw everywhere, most of it being committed by Tommy and Dallas.

We all met in the foyer of the Hilton and stood open-mouthed in absolute awe. The foyer was filled with marble, the fittings were gold, and elegant, multi-coloured flamingos pranced around. Magnificent. Magnificent is also the word I'd use to describe the tackle that Tommy Raudonikis put on one of these poor creatures. And then, as usual, he went too far by pulling the flamingo's head clean off!

The patrons of this splendid hotel screamed in horror as our captain, realising that what was good clean fun around Lidcombe way might not suit snooty Manhattan, attempted to mop up the bird's blood with his hanky and the concierge's face. We were outraged when the manager of the Hilton cancelled our accommodation on the spot and threw us out into the mean streets of New York. Yanks have no sense of humour!

We were screwed. Nowhere to go, nowhere to stay. Then

I remembered Dad telling me before we left Australia that if I had a few days spare I should get on a train and pay a visit to Great-Uncle Ron, who was living in Washington. I had Ron's number in my pocket, and while I didn't want to impose, things were pretty desperate for the boys and me.

Anyway, I made the call and you wouldn't believe it, Ron's butler answered and told me I needed to make an appointment just to speak to the stuck-up prick. I let the butler have both barrels: 'You go tell your f**kin' boss his nephew Reg is on the phone, Benson.'

In no time, Great-Uncle Ron was on the other end of the line and, to be honest, he sounded like a decent fella. I told him the mess we were in. He said he understood, and that my friends and I were welcome to come to Washington and stay at his joint. Even when I told him that my friends were a touring party of Rugby League footballers, he chuckled and said, 'Reg, the more the merrier!' I asked him for the address of his house and he said not to worry, there'd be a fleet of limousines waiting for us at the train station. Geez, I thought to myself, Ron must be doing OK.

The train journey from Grand Central Station to Washington was total chaos. The boys trashed every compartment and it was a bloody miracle we reached our destination without being thrown off. I couldn't blame the fellas. There was no booze on the train and that trip was the first time any of us had been sober since the season ended six weeks before.

True to Great-Uncle Ron's word, at Washington station a line of gleaming black limos was waiting, and they whisked us off in black-leather luxury to Ron's joint.

I was still a little worried about how he was going to be able to put up 20 blokes. Maybe he'd pitch some tents in his backyard, or a bunch of us could sleep in his tool shed. But as we rounded a corner, we pulled into the driveway of the most magnificent mansion I have ever seen. It was all white and there were heavily armed security men crawling all over it. I asked our driver, 'Mate, is Great-Uncle Ronny a drug dealer?'

He saluted me and snapped out, military-style, 'No, sir! Your great-uncle is the President of the United States!'

I laughed in his face. 'Ah, so he's *that* Ronald Reagan! Well, f**k me.'

The boys were hooting and hollering as they all jumped out of their limos. On the great lawn a few started up a game of touch with one of the cushions from their limo, and nearly collided with dear old Great-Uncle Ron and his ugly missus, Nancy, who were there to greet us. I walked up to Ron and gave him a big hug. It sure was great to catch up with family.

The president invited us all in and sent his flunkies off to fetch two dozen cartons of KB from his private stash. You can take the boy out of Cessnock, but you can't take Cessnock out of the boy!

For the rest of the night we all sat around the Oval Office with our feet up on a desk that had once belonged to George Washington, drinking piss and listening to Led Zeppelin. Ron loved the boys. It was obvious Great-Aunty Nancy did too. I caught her with her tongue down Graeme O'Grady's throat on more than a few occasions. Ron just laughed it off, he was in high spirits. His favourite nephew was in town.

We partied right through the night and Uncle Ron formed a real bond with Tommy Raudonikis. He was fascinated by Tom's attitude to foreign policy. 'Just kill the f**kin' wogs,' was Tom's solution to bringing peace to all the troublespots of the world.

THIS IS MY LIFE!

Ron's butler took the rest of the boys on a tour of the White House. Bobby introduced the First Couple to humour Magpie-style by dropping a huge turd under their bed. John Dorahy was sprung trying to call 0500 numbers on the presidential phone.

Our stay at the White House was truly inspiring. We'd planned to leave after the weekend, but Ron and Nancy begged us to stay. We were reluctant, but how do you say no to the President of the United States? The last thing we wanted was Nancy to have to get down on her knees and plead. All of us except O'Grady, of course.

So we stayed on, and as a special request Ron asked us to accompany him to a very important meeting that day in downtown Washington. He asked 10 of us to be his security team. He explained in the limo into town that he was a bit freaked out because some arsehole had been sending threatening letters to the White House. When we reached the conference centre we all piled inside.

The meeting was an important one, a War On Drugs summit. I'll never forget how great it was just to sit there at the back of the hall enjoying a beer and the occasional cigarette while listening to these world leaders exchanging views. Russia's president, Boris Yeltsin, demanded a no-tolerance policy on drugs. British prime minister Margaret Thatcher called for a trade ban to be imposed on Colombia. Great-Uncle Ron wanted tougher checks at the border controls. Tommy Raudonikis kept screaming, 'Kill the f**kin' wogs!' Inspiring stuff.

At the end of the meeting, which went for seven hours, all the Wests guys were pretty tanked and, with hindsight, probably a bit lax about protecting Ron. Anyway, as we all stepped out of the building onto the footpath, this lunatic came flying out of the crowd and opened fire on my poor uncle.

The bullets hit him in the shoulder. Then Dallas Donnelly took control. He kicked Ron up the arse and into his limo to safety. The assassin tried to flee but he was no match for Tommy, Les, Bobby Cooper and me. We grabbed the jerk, knocked his gun away and then used his face as a punching bag and his hair for toilet paper. Turns out we'd nabbed the wrong fella, but the police commissioner took his hiding with good humour. After a long chase we finally apprehended the shooter, and in true Magpie style, mustered the energy to pound his face black and blue . . . The bloke's name was John Hinckley. He has gone down in history as the man who tried to assassinate President Ronald Reagan. Without the boys from Western Suburbs, I have no doubt he'd be remembered today as the bloke who *killed* the president.

While Great-Uncle Ron was being operated on, we all went back to the White House to drink more piss. We didn't know it as we got stuck into the KB, but we had become the heroes of America. We would all receive awards for bravery, and were grilled about our heroism on CNN and all the other major networks.

Ron made a total recovery and showered us with gifts, including flying us all over America to see the sights. We partied at the Playboy Mansion, pissed off the side of the Golden Gate Bridge and ran nude through Disneyland. Yes, sir, this was a never-to-be-forgotten trip.

Finally, we flew home to Sydney first class as 'friends' of American Airlines. We disembarked as a bunch of young blokes high on life and as close-knit as a team could be. Who could have known that dark clouds were looming?

9
SACKED

JUST A WEEK BEFORE pre-season training began, Roy called me into his office for a special meeting. It turned out media magnate John Singleton had lured our skipper, Tommy Raudonikis, to the Newtown Jets with big bucks and Roy was deeply concerned that Tom was going to leave a hole we couldn't fill.

Roy explained to me that Tommy was more than just a beer pig and human smoke machine, he was an inspiration. Roy needed a bloke to take the big step up and be the new Tommy. 'That man is you, Reg,' said Roy. 'I name you the new captain of the Magpies club.'

I was so excited that as soon as I got home I called Mum and Dad. Mum congratulated me and said how much I deserved the honour after my great commitment to Wests the year before. Dad by this time, unfortunately, had started

The Cessnock Truth

REG REAGAN SACKED!

CESSNOCK WOMAN GIVES BIRTH TO HAIRY TRIPLETS!

EVENING EDITION

It was the day man walked on the moon, but something else dominated the headlines in ol' Cessnock town.

to lose his mind after 50 solid years of pissing-up. All the old bastard did these days was dress up in Mum's lingerie and listen to Leo Sayer CDs. But, nonetheless, he was excited by my great news and told me I made him feel like dancin'.

I, of course, played it down big-time in the media, but to be perfectly honest, I was turning f**kin' cartwheels and set myself a goal. I would be as good a skipper as Tom Raudonikis, if not better!

Roy assured me I had the support of all my teammates and I believed they were behind me to a man. Then, out of nowhere, a headline hit me like a Mack truck. I was filling up my new sponsored Nissan Bluebird and when I went into the servo to pay, I glanced down at the pile of newspapers and read on the front page: 'We Won't Cop Reg As Club Captain – Unnamed Wests Players'.

I was shocked and horrified, but quickly figured that the malcontents must have been some under-23s players jealous of my rise. I raced the Bluebird over to where the 23s were training and told them they had no worries about me being their captain, because unless I lost an arm or a leg, I wouldn't be playing alongside them in Z Grade.

Their smartarse captain, Snoopy Williams, who always had a bad word for me after he caught me in bed with his girlfriend, sister and mother, piped up and told me to f**k off. 'That's no way to speak to the club captain,' I replied while I reversed the Bluebird backwards and forwards over his head. That taught Snoopy a thing or two about respecting his betters.

Later that night I got a call from the journo who wrote the article. He wouldn't tell me his name and I couldn't pick his voice because either he had a handkerchief over the phone or he was going down on his missus at the time. He mumbled that there was indeed serious discontent among the first graders about my promotion. They reckoned I thought I was better than them and always demanded and got special treatment from club management.

The thing was, I didn't *think* I was better than all the boys. I *knew* I was, and therefore deserved as much special treatment as could be mustered.

Next day I headed down to training with a serious bee in my bonnet. I knew I held all the aces because without me Wests were a club of shit-kickers. So, rather than reason with the boys, I took a deep breath, sucked my nuts up into my guts and let fly with a good 20-minute spray at my low-life, untalented, ungrateful brothers in arms. My theme: accept me as your fearless leader or tell me to piss off.

Roy and the boys hung their heads. They knew I was right in everything I said. They knew we'd been through so much together. They knew they needed me more than they needed oxygen, or even beer. But that didn't stop them from telling me to f**k off.

I was shattered. I fell to my knees on the Lidcombe Oval turf. I cried fake tears. I pleaded with them to take me back. I offered them money, free beer, oral sex. But it was no good, my fate was sealed. So, rather than lose my dignity, I stopped kissing Roy's feet, got up off my knees, spun on my heel and walked off the oval for the last time.

I drove straight to some sleazy little pub and sat at the bar for two or three weeks. I fell into a deep, deep depression. Many chief executives and coaches of rival clubs dropped in to have a drink and try to persuade me to join their team. Even so, I felt like the loneliest man in the world. With the possible exception of Molly Meldrum.

THIS IS MY LIFE!

Finally, one morning as I sat staring into the bottom of my schooner glass feeling sorry for myself, I had a vision. It was time for old Reg to return to his roots. I had become lost in the big city and it was time to go back to the life that had made me the living legend I was.

I rolled off my bar stool, ordered a six-pack to go, collected up the only belongings I had left in the world – a beer cooler, some old footy boots and my pair of Levi Strauss bell-bottoms – and walked off into the glorious sunshine determined to make myself an even better man.

10
BRING BACK THE BUSH

As I wandered about in all that glorious sunshine I realised I truly didn't have a f**kin' clue what I was doing or where I was going. I must have looked like I was homeless, which, funnily enough, I was.

After strolling aimlessly for two days I decided to take a seat on a park bench. It was a windy afternoon and newspapers danced past me as I sat there glumly. Then fate blew a copy of *Rugby League Week* right against my leg. It was the November issue and there I was on the front cover under the heading: 'Greatest Ever?' Reading my own press was always a passion of mine and, like alcohol, often soothed my troubled soul. So I grasped the magazine and flicked through it.

About three or four pages in, I glanced at an advertisement that read: 'The West Tamworth Robins have a vacancy

'Nice fiddle'. Tamworth used me in their big 1980s tourism push. It did the trick. The next year this ol' country town had more overseas visitors than New York. Ninety per cent of them were women. Geez, I wonder why.

for a first-grade captain–coach. No experience required but preferred. If interested, call the leagues club.' I reached into the pocket of my stubbies and with the last of my loose change, I made the momentous phone call.

The bloke from the Robins nearly dropped dead when I told him who I was and that I was applying for the captain–coach's job. He explained to me that I'd have to sit for an interview and then my application would be weighed against the many other aspirants'. But I could hear in the background, already blasting over the club's PA system, the announcement: 'Ladies and gentlemen, I have urgent news. Reg Reagan will be captain–coach of the Robins this year. You f**kin' beauty! Free piss for everyone for the next two hours!' I had a feeling the job was mine.

The Robins sent a car to Sydney to take me to West Tamworth. They had entrusted their football club to me. When I arrived, I saw a huge sign that read, 'Tamworth – The Home of Country Music and Reg Reagan.'

Next day, the council organised a motorcade for me. From behind the thick Perspex windows of my bulletproof enclosure, I directed my minder to pass onto the townsfolk my wish that they all accept me as just another citizen of their lovely village.

The community used my image in a big tourism push. I posed naked next to the Big Guitar in an advertisement. The copy underneath the photo said, 'Come to Tamworth and fiddle with Our Two Finest Instruments'.

I loved the people of this gorgeous rural region and my popularity, in turn, was enormous. So popular was I, that I had to put two security guards out the front of my house with instructions to shoot anyone who ventured onto my lawn.

Being captain–coach of the Robins was a ball. I was my own boss. This meant I had to be disciplined, so, to prove I was serious about the job, I always made sure I turned up for the last 10 minutes of every second training session. It gave me a tremendous sense of wellbeing to praise a young player and watch his self-esteem grow. Even more enjoyable was seeing their heads drop after a typical Reg Reagan bollocking.

Then, one night, something happened that changed my life forever. I was at the local having a few beers with the boys when into the pub walked the most beautiful and seductive woman I had ever seen. I immediately told the fellas that one day she would be my wife. I was transfixed by this gorgeous woman. Suddenly I was unable to hear the racket of voices in the bar or Feargal Sharkey singing on the jukebox.

'Go on, Reg,' I told myself. 'Walk over and ask her out.' And with that, I took one swig of my schooner and strode across. 'Would you like to come to the movies with me?' I asked this stunning vision.

'Aw, go and get f**ked!' she replied.

So instead I asked out her rather plain friend, Ruth, and I'm proud to say that we're still together to this day.

Apart from the odd stray root, Ruth and I were inseparable. In no time flat I knew she was the one for me. Sure, she was built like a Sherman tank and obviously suffered from an allergic reaction to deodorant, but Ruthie was a good sport. She could keep up with me schooner for schooner, and she loved her footy. A few years back she had even been the Robins' head cheerleader and by all reports was the town bike. But who hasn't got a past?

The Robins' season was going great. We were flying high at the top of the table, a fair achievement considering we'd been wooden spooners the year before. The football, of course, was a level or two down from what I was used to and I could have played most games wearing a dinner suit. In fact, that's exactly what I wore in one game against Armidale, just to show them what a bunch of untalented fools they were.

Other teams' fans cheered me louder than their own guys and most matches ended with me being shouldered in triumph from the field. I began to understand how Julius Caesar must have felt.

It was no surprise when I was asked to captain–coach Country Firsts against City, and apparently inspired a rare victory over the Sydneysiders. I say 'apparently' because I didn't actually bother turning up – it seems that just seeing my name alongside theirs in the program was enough to make the Country fellas burst with pride and give it to the City poofters.

Taking advantage of my popularity in Tamworth, I released a single just in time for that year's Country Music Festival. It was called 'My Life Among Mortals' and it shot straight to No. 1 in Australia and East Germany. When the Berlin Wall was finally pulled down, the German government flew me over to perform my song in the main square. It was a deeply emotional moment for all the citizens of the newly united Germany. But right after my performance I pissed right off. I couldn't wait to get away from those sauerkraut-gobblers. Their snags tasted like shit, their beer was woeful, their sheilas were hairier than me. But the trip did its job and, soon after, 'My Life Among Mortals' went double platinum and won me a Golden Guitar and a Grammy nomination.

THIS IS MY LIFE!

I arrived back home just as the semifinals were heating up, and I scored four tries against Armidale to take the Robins into their first grand final in 10 years.

Grand-final week was fabulous and it was good to see the town getting behind the whole team, not just me as usual. We were up against our archrivals, Kempsey, who brought a fair contingent of support with them to the game. But there was never any doubt who enjoyed majority support and Scully Park was dripping in the Robins' colours.

The match was an anticlimax. We dominated from the start and won 42–12. I scored six tries – four of them length-of-the-field efforts – and converted every one. After the game I was presented with the Reg Reagan Trophy for being the best player on the field.

That night the club really rocked and I was invited up on stage to say a few words. The place went berserk as I strolled across the auditorium. The punters started the old chant, 'Reggy Reagan is a god – doo-dah, doo-dah, Reggie Reagan is a god – oh, the doo-dah day!' It was a great gesture and, to be fair, not far from the truth. But as I neared the podium, I knew there were a few little issues I needed to get off my chest.

Once on stage I told them to shut the f**k up because I wanted to speak. 'Firstly,' I began, 'I'm pretty pissed off that sales of my single in Tamworth haven't met my expectations. Here I am, giving you bastards my blood and guts and it wouldn't f**kin' kill you to fork out twenty-five dollars to buy my CD! But no, you're all too bloody selfish and would rather spend your money on bread, milk and clean water! As far as I'm concerned, you've given me a huge kick in the nuts and to return the favour I'm moving on.' Just before I left the stage, I remembered to thank the townspeople for chipping in and buying me a gold Rolex as a gesture of thanks, and I wished them all the best in their future endeavours.

A few drunken idiots tried to ruin the night by jeering me from the stage, but they were put in their place real quick, Reg Reagan-style. I guess some people just can't take constructive criticism.

I left town that night. I was like the Chuck Norris of Rugby League, never ready to settle in one place because there was always a greater challenge over the next hill. I loaded my trophy, my Rolex and Ruthie into the back seat of the trusty Bluebird and set off for greener pastures.

11
FAMILY MAN

SIX MONTHS LATER, I was up the coast starring for the Burleigh Heads Bears when I decided to change my life forever. By now I was sick and tired of playing the field. I'd learned that having beautiful women throwing themselves at me every day wasn't all it was cracked up to be. It was becoming boring and I was ready to do something about it.

One night I asked Ruth to come for a walk, and we stretched our stumpy legs on the beautiful beach until we stopped to rest on the headland at Burleigh Heads. The night was magnificent. There wasn't a hint of a breeze, not a trace of humidity, and the ocean was so still I could see my reflection in its surface. Ruth could tell I had something important to say to her, and she encouraged me to hurry up and spit it out so she could go back to drinking schooners with the blokes at the surf club.

Me and Ruthie, just seconds before we were hammered by hailstones.

So, while butterflies fluttered in my guts, I took a deep, deep breath and asked this loving, but plain, woman if she would marry me. She thoughtfully ran her fingers through her oily hair, dragged deeply on her Alpine and romantically replied: 'Yeah, why not! Now it's your f**kin' shout!' We embraced, and suddenly the heavens opened and hailstones the size of a German shepherd's nutbag hammered down upon us from the skies. We ran back to the surf club with blood streaming down our faces and I knew it was a sign from the gods that Ruth and I were a match made in heaven.

Our wedding was, simply, a dream, mainly because I was so pissed I fell asleep at the altar. But from what I can remember of it, it was one of the great days. My wedding party comprised a couple of my old Wests Magpies buddies, Bobby Cooper and Les Boyd; Lord Mayor of Burleigh, Ducky Thompson; a few of the West Tamworth Robins lads; and Bert and Patti Newton. My best man? No prizes for guessing it was Tommy Raudonikis, even though he was still full from the night before and forgot to turn up.

On the day my Ruthie looked absolutely respectable in her black dress. Even her dog-ugly crew of bridesmaids nearly crept into the not-bad category.

The wedding ceremony went off pretty much without a hitch and the reception was a wonderful occasion. We chose Meatloaf's 'Bat Out Of Hell' as our wedding waltz and there was hardly a dry eye in the place as we drove off into the night finally married... with Tommy, having finally appeared, passed out – paralytic pissed, tied to the back bumper of our old Bluebird. You'd like to think you only get married once, so I splashed out on our honeymoon and we spent four days and five nights in beautiful Lithgow.

We wasted no time starting a family and today we have three wonderful kids, Reg Jnr, Randy and Rick. I love being a father and passing on the lessons of life to the young 'uns. Reg Jnr is a real chip off the old block. He enjoys screwing sheilas and drinking piss. He turns 13 next week and I've already ordered the strippers for his party.

Randy is just as his name suggests. Already I can hear through the paper-thin walls of the Reagan mansion the sounds of the dirty little bastard jerking off. Randy can't decide whether to be a fashion designer, a rock star or a plumber. I urge him to do all three if he can find the time. Randy is only 11 but very mature for his age. He used to go to all the nightclubs in and around our area. I had to set him straight, and tell him these cesspools of sleaze and debauchery were no place for one so young and innocent. Now he sticks to the RSL.

The baby of the family is Rick. He's only nine but already a big boy (and I'm not talking about height). Rick is a lot more sensitive than my other two no-hopers and doesn't really get involved in sport or macho things. He doesn't even drink! The kid is everything I'm not. Ruth and I call him our Miracle Child because he came into our life two years after I had my vasectomy.

I'm teaching my children to grow up the right way. Get an education, respect your elders, always wear a rubber if you're not serious about the sheila. I'm very aware that kids are the future of Australia, and so by bringing mine up Reg Reagan-style I'm making this world of ours a far better place.

Being my kids is not easy for Reg Jnr, Randy and Rick. The expectations of them are many and huge, whether they're sitting for a maths exam, playing soccer on Saturdays or undressing for a shower after gym class. Realising this, I always tell my sons to do what their dad has done: live their own life and not worry about what others say.

My family has grown accustomed to me being linked romantically to just about every glamorous woman who has graced the silver screen, and while Ruth and the boys know I'm faithful (except when I'm not), this doesn't necessarily make life in my shadow any easier for them. Poor Rick comes home from school in tears some days after schoolmates have teased him about his dad dating Halle Berry or Michelle Pfeiffer. I guess I'm partly to blame for this scuttlebutt. Maybe I should never have taken Halle and Michelle to parent–teacher night.

It's one of the burdens of my greatness that I have to live an exemplary life as a family man and be a role model for my kids and *all* the children of Australia. You know, I wouldn't have it any other way.

12

BAGGY GREEN GUT

LET ME JUST STATE for the record, Mr Chairman (this is something I say in front of mixed company to make me sound even more important and quite intelligent), I bloody *love* the game of cricket.

I have had very few regrets in my long and successful life, but for a while there I had a nagging feeling, particularly after scoring one of my regular centuries against the piss-poor medium pace of Randy in our backyard cricket matches, that I was crash-hot enough at the grand old game to have excelled at the very top level.

Problem was, I'd never had the chance to put myself to the test. When you're super-multi-talented, and always being chosen to represent Australia in one sport or another, some games slip through the cracks. And with all my Rugby League and Union, surfing, boxing and tenpin bowling

'So that's it?' I always dreamed of scoring a test century. Once I did it, I couldn't believe how easy it was.

commitments, I'd neglected the willow and six stitcher. One day it occurred to old Reg that while cricket, as an international sport, was much the poorer for my absence, I just didn't know how to break in.

But put your hankies away. Thanks to a weird twist of fate, I did get the opportunity to prove to myself and the world that my suspicion I possessed true cricketing greatness was not unfounded. Here's how it happened . . .

Like all red-blooded, heterosexual males there's nothing I've enjoyed more in life than going down to the old Sydney Cricket Ground and watching a good day's play while ripping into the piss. I do it to this day, but it's nothing compared to the incredible high I used to get on the old SCG Hill, before it was levelled, sitting with Reg Jnr, Randy and Rick, hurling abuse at out-of-form Windies and pommy batsmen, soft-cock medium pace Kiwi bowlers and catch-dropping curry-munchers from the Subcontinent. Many's the time I'd entertain the faithful throng with such razor-sharp witticisms as 'Kill that black West Indian bastard!' and 'Hey, Sunil, show us ya turban!' The crowd loved it. My kids did too. In a strange way, it made me feel more Australian.

Some people think I'm a fickle supporter, but that's not true. I'm very consistent. Every time the pricks don't get any runs, I turn on them.

It was a glorious afternoon just a few years ago, day one of the first test between Australia and Pakistan, and I was giving Mark 'Tubby' Taylor a heavy roast. The Tubster was smack in the middle of a lengthy dry spell with the bat, and because he was the Aussie captain I made sure my insults were especially scathing.

Anyway, as I expected it would, Taylor's wicket again fell

cheaply. Time for the Reg-meister to give him both barrels. From my possie in the concourse, I called Tubby every name under the sun. At one stage of my brilliant tirade he even sneaked a peek in my direction, trying to single out his tormentor. When our eyes met, I dropped my pants and bared my hairy white arse. 'Hey, Mudguts!' I yelled. 'How ya seein' 'em today? See if you can hit this.' Even from 80 metres away I could tell he was red-faced with fury, but I felt safe deep in the crowd.

By the fourth day, the test seemed headed for a draw. Not that I cared. I was three KBs off paralytic and my repertoire of dick tricks was getting huge cheers from the crowd. Suddenly, right in the middle of a particularly demanding trick, a gruff voice barked at me, 'Hey, arse-wipe!' It was Taylor standing on the boundary holding cap, bat, pads, gloves and protector. 'You reckon you're the expert. Why don't you open the batting instead of me and see if you can do better!'

I didn't need a second invitation. I put away my dick, zipped up my fly and leapt over the fence. Grabbing Taylor's willow, I cried, 'Get out of my way!' I threw on all the gear as I made my way to the crease. The crowd was going berserk. The bat felt great in my hands, Tubby's cap, pads and gloves fitted perfectly, but his hector protector was agonisingly too tight!

My opening partner was the flashy Mark Waugh, who had the nerve to suggest to me that I should use a helmet. 'Stick it up your arse! I don't need a skullcap to hide *my* dandruff, pretty boy!' I told him.

I could hardly believe it. Here I was in the centre of the packed Sydney Cricket Ground, wearing the baggy green cap of my country, about to face the lightning pace of Wasim Akram and Waqar Younis, when only minutes before I was just another bloke in the crowd (although one with his dick over his left wrist and his scrotum stretched across the rim of a schooner glass). Life's funny like that . . .

Akram took the ball and was motoring in at me from the Randwick end when I decided it was time to play ducks and drakes. Just as the great quick bowler was about to let the ball go, I stepped away from the crease and told umpire Dickie Bird that I wanted the sight screen adjusted. Akram ground to a screaming halt. The seventh time I did this, Wasim had the nerve to blow up. Fair dinkum, those curry-munchers can't take a joke.

And it wasn't just Akram who had a humour bypass. Can you believe that Bird gave me an official warning for conduct contrary to the spirit of cricket? Again, my wit saved the situation. 'Aw, f**k off,' I replied, 'and think about having a shower, you smelly pommy bastard!' When Dickie threatened to report me to the match referee, I simply pointed out that he should be ashamed of himself for taking Akram's side. Only nine months before we'd been at war with these bludgers. It did me little good.

By then, the injustice of it all was really pissing me off and, let me tell you, an angry Reg Reagan is a dangerous Reg Reagan.

When Akram finally got to bowl a ball at me, he was so frustrated he over-pitched it slightly. I paid it the respect it deserved and smashed it to the boundary. The crowd went berserk, and stayed at fever pitch for the next 40 minutes as I continued my assault on the bowlers and belted 74 majestic runs, giving those Pakis a taste of their own vindaloo!

At the tea break I strode from the SCG to a standing ovation. Every person there was on his feet. Hats, children and domestic animals were thrown high into the air. I only stopped bowing and waving my cap when I saw my batting partner, Mark Waugh, making for me, his hand outstretched, pathetically desperate to make himself look a big man by joining in the congratulations. I stopped Waugh cold with a gesture of my own. 'Want a piggypack, mate?' I snapped. 'After all, I've been bloody carrying you all session!' The crowd picked up on the jibe, and began a deafening chant, 'Junior's a wanker!' It was music to my ears.

As I reached the boundary, half a dozen sheilas started groping me, asking me to sign their tits. I obliged. How could I disappoint the selectors' wives?

In the change room, Australian coach Geoff Marsh asked me what I wanted during the interval. 'A banana sandwich, some Gatorade, a piece of fruit?' he suggested. I gave him my order and in no time the slab of KB, carton of Winfields and the strippers arrived.

What a memory. Sitting in the famous SCG change room with four naked pole dancers using my body as a jumping castle, I soon got a feel for the history of the place. On the walls were photos of the Don, Keith Miller and Scott Muller. I was sure in great company and I don't mind saying I became a little emotional.

My nostalgic reverie was broken when Marsh told me play was about to recommence. Soon I was back out in the middle, giving those Pakis another hammering. I reached my century to wild applause and a Mexican wave. During tea I'd taken the chance to have a word in the ear of the official scorer, and he didn't let me down. When I lofted Younis into the third tier of the Brewongle Stand to bring up my ton, the electronic scoreboard, in an unprecedented gesture, flashed the words: 'Reg Reagan – 100 runs. Stick that up your fat arse, Tubby!'

The SCG went nuts and the famous ground suddenly exploded with a crowd invasion of monumental proportions. Well-wishers were slapping me on the back, hoisting me on their shoulders, stroking my genital region. It was total chaos for a good 25 minutes.

At last sanity was restored and, shortly after, I was dubiously dismissed for a slashing 131.

Next day I was the toast of the cricket world. 'Reagan Serves Up Delicious Curry' declared the *Daily Telegraph*. 'A Star Is Born!' exclaimed the *Herald-Sun*. 'Reg Labels Pakis Poofters' headlined the *Pakistani Times*. I had arrived.

The rest of the Aussies were unable to uphold my high standards, and I was forced to watch in angry frustration as our batting collapsed. In spite of my heroic dig, Australia lost the test. Not that I gave a shit by then. I was too busy enjoying the hospitality of the members stand. There was one unfortunate incident, when some bloke named Bill Lawry took exception to me putting the weights on his missus. I took him outside and splattered the bastard's enormous snotbox all over his face. There's nothing uglier than a jealous husband.

That night I went out for some celebratory drinks. That lasted a week or so. My partying was interrupted by a call from some dickhead named Trevor Hohns, who informed me that because of my fine form against Pakistan I had been selected to tour the West Indies with the Aussies. My initial response was to tell Hohns to stick it up his arse, because the Rugby League season was about to kick off. But after a bit more thought, I figured that my contract negotiations with the South Queensland Crushers were going nowhere, so I told Hohns: 'OK, mate, I'm in. I wouldn't mind a Caribbean holiday.'

I hurried home and packed my bags. I kissed the missus and kids goodbye. 'See you in two months!' I yelled as I hailed a cab to the airport.

The Aussie team was already at Kingsford-Smith, and before we flew out we had to front at a media conference where each of us was asked in turn about the upcoming tour. Mark Taylor spoke of the grand tradition of the Frank Worrell Trophy, and what winning it would mean to the entire team and the Australian nation. Then Steve Waugh stood up and, with a steely look in his eye, told how ruthless and tough those Windies players were.

Then it was my turn. Now, I have one golden rule when I deal with the press: speak from the heart. Cricket journo Robert Craddock posed the question: 'Mr Reagan, what are your personal goals for the tour?' Fair question, and I answered as honestly as I could, 'Play a bit of cricket, drink a bit of piss, bed a lot of sheilas.'

The TV reporters frantically tried to erase the videotape before it could be beamed back to the networks, and the press journos began shouting at me, asking if I'd really said what they'd thought I'd said. 'Bloody oath, I did!' I cried as all hell broke loose.

Suddenly this grey-headed weasel jumped up in front of me screaming: 'No, he didn't mean that! He didn't mean it!'

I was angry now. 'Sit down! No one speaks for Reg Reagan!'

Unfortunately, the weasel turned out to ACB chairman Malcolm Speed, who wanted to boot me off the tour until the calmer heads of Steve Waugh and Mark Taylor prevailed. Tugga and Tubby told Speed in no uncertain terms that without me, the Aussies had as much chance as a snowball in Trinidad of winning a single match, let alone the Frank Worrell Trophy. 'Oh, OK then,' said a humbled Speed, 'Reagan is still on the tour, but one more black mark against his name and he's on the plane home.'

The flight to Jamaica was fantastic. I knew a few of the stewardesses from my previous Kangaroo tours, so they were aware I liked my KB cold and constant. I even made the Mile High Club a few times with a strapping good-looker with fair hair. Over our post-coital Winfield I suggested it might be best if we both kept our sexual escapade on the hush-hush. Happily, Matt Hayden agreed.

We stopped over in LA and then, for the final leg down to the Caribbean, the team doctor gave us all a few sleeping tablets. He said if we took one straight away and the rest before we landed in the West Indies, we'd get plenty of sleep and avoid jet lag. Only Ricky Ponting and I refused to swallow the tablets. Now, what's a sporting tour without a resident prankster? And who better to play the joker than old Reg? When the boys had dozed off, I went through their pockets and stole the remaining sleeping pills.

I took the empty seat next to Ponting. 'C'mon, Punter,' I whispered in his ear, 'let's rip into the piss while the other blokes are out of it. More for us!' 'You bet, Reggie,' said Punter. Then, while he was distracted asking the stewardess for something to munch on, I dropped 12 sleeping pills into his KB can. 'Now, skoll that!' I cried.

The tablets kicked in faster than I expected. In 10 minutes, Ponting was snoring. I seized my chance and shaved off both his eyebrows, then jammed chunks of Moroccan chicken up his nose. Christ, it was hilarious.

When the rest of the team woke up, they took one look at Punter and, like me, laughed themselves silly. It was the funniest thing any of us had ever seen until Ponting, the soft bastard, began foaming at the mouth. Then we laughed harder.

The team doctor rushed over and asked me what was wrong with him. 'Don't know, Doc. Could be the flu or maybe he's one of these guys who can't handle their beer,' I replied as tears of mirth rolled down my cheeks. The doctor took Punter's pulse and when he couldn't find it, ordered the pilot to make an emergency landing in Cancún, Mexico, where Ricky had his stomach pumped at the hospital and was interviewed by police about his suspected addiction to sleeping tablets.

Punter remained on a drip all the rest of our flight to Jamaica, but his discomfort was forgotten when we landed at the airport and were met by a horde of cheering fans and media. As I was about to disembark, Malcolm Speed read me the riot act, saying, 'Now, Reg, I don't want any more trouble.' I replied, 'Mal, you've got nothing to worry about with me.'

On the tarmac, reporters ignored the Waughs, Taylor and Warney and rushed up to yours truly. 'Mr Reagan, what's your first impression of Jamaica?' they all yelled in unison. 'Lots of Aborigines,' I replied.

I must say that when it comes to the great cities of the world, I'm a hard bloke to please. I've been to plenty

... London, Paris, Rome, Mudgee. But Jamaica was something else. The people were so friendly, and when they mobbed me, all smiles and handshakes, every single one reeked of booze, even the kids. I was impressed.

At the team hotel, Tubby Taylor told me I'd be opening the batting in our first match the next day, against the West Indies A side. I was too pissed to be excited, and decided to hit the town to celebrate.

The Jamaicans warmed to me instantly. All it took to win them over was a bit of bullshit about how I'd been a great mate of the late Bob Marley. The gullible bastards bought me rum after rum, but because I had a big game to play, I said my farewells and returned to the hotel early, at about 4 am. I flopped into bed as the room revolved like a merry-go-round in overdrive.

My roomie was the big Queensland fast bowler Carl Rackemann. Like me, Rackers is a bloke who's partial to his piss, so it was a match made in heaven. Carl tipped me out of bed just in time to board the team bus to the ground.

Somehow, in spite of me going easy on the booze the night before, I seemed to be half-pissed. And I felt a bit crook. Must have been the meat-lover's pizza I ate for breakfast. What I needed was the hair of the dog. I climbed onto the team bus, KB in hand. 'This bus is an alcohol-free zone,' said Mr Killjoy extraordinaire Malcolm Speed. I could easily have demolished him with my wit, but sometimes action speaks louder than words. Much louder. I grabbed Speed in a headlock that Stone Cold Steve Austin would have been proud of. Then I forced his face into my arse and let rip an Olympic-sized fart fuelled by KB, overproof rum and pizza with nine different kinds of meat.

Speed screamed and broke my grip. To the cheers of us all, he crawled off the bus and fell in a heap on the roadside. He lay there twitching and dry-retching for nearly half an hour as the boys chanted, 'Reg-gie! Reg-gie! Reg-gie!' It was just like old times, and I whispered to myself, 'You've still got it, old boy!'

The match against West Indies A was a good one – for the team, and especially for my good self. I scored a swashbuckling 72 off as many balls and would've cracked my second consecutive ton in the baggy green cap if I hadn't got bored shitless and purposely stepped on my stumps.

That night, Tubby, Rackers, Warney and I went out for a few beers. I continued to make friends, with my bullshit stories and good-natured womanising.

The Aussie side played a few more warm-up matches and then came the time for the first test team to be named. At the meeting when the names were to be announced, I felt super-confident I'd be the first man picked. I positioned myself at the front of the room so I could check out the disappointment on the faces of the poor bastards who'd missed out.

It was Tubby Taylor's job to read out the test XI and, to my disbelief and horror, I was named 12th man. I reckoned there were two ways to take news like that. I could carry on like a pork chop, or accept it like a gentleman, knowing what doesn't kill you makes you stronger. I took it like a pork chop. 'You evil, fat bastard, Taylor!' I raged. 'I've obviously been sucking the wrong dicks!'

Taylor tried to cut me off, 'Now then, Reg, cop it on the chin.' 'F**k that!' I yelled at the skipper, 'Cop *this* on the chin!' and I delivered a perfectly executed right uppercut that knocked Taylor cold. I was about to drag him to his feet and let him have another one, when Warney pinioned my arms behind me. 'Leave him, mate,' he said, 'he's had enough.'

I have to say in Tubby's favour that he took his hiding like a man, and when they unwired his jaw he apologised to me from his hospital bed for the miserable way I'd been treated. I decided to let bygones be bygones and that I would make the most of my 12th man duties. You know, fire the boys up with inspirational pep talks, maybe break the tension with a bit of comic relief, and get paralytically drunk every night.

On the opening day of the first test I rose to the challenge and came up with some classic Reg Reagan humour just when it was needed most. A now-fully recovered Mark Taylor (who was occupying my rightful position at first drop) and Michael Slater were mounting a solid opening partnership in the blazing West Indian sun. Suddenly, Taylor started swaying all over the pitch and calling to me to bring him a drink. My medical training told me he was suffering from dehydration. Naturally, like any good 12th man, I was prepared for every emergency and rushed out to my captain with a water bottle.

Taylor snatched the bottle from me and had skolled almost a litre of my urine before he collapsed on the wicket vomiting uncontrollably. I was doubled up on the ground too. He'd fallen hook, line and sinker for this great old trick I learned in my bush footy days. 'Now we're square, Tubby,' I howled. Tubby, though crook, saw the funny side later on.

At the end of the day's play I caught up with a few old Aussie greats who were in the West Indies hosting supporters' tours. That night Alan Border, Greg Matthews and I went out to sink a few. I can honestly say this was one of *the* best nights of my life. Great company, plenty of rum and good

THIS IS MY LIFE!

music. It was only a matter of time before Mo Matthews asked me if I'd like to share a smoke with him.

'OK, mate,' I said, confused. I had never seen someone make such a big deal of having an innocent Winnie Red. I must admit, though, that these cigarettes certainly had a strange taste. Must be the way they make 'em over here, I thought. I shrugged and had a few more puffs . . .

The rest of the night was a blur. My form on the dance floor was hot, and sheilas were hanging off me everywhere as the reggae took me to another world. Suddenly I was aware of the floor rushing to meet my face and all went black.

Next thing I knew, it was morning and I was in a bed lying between Brian Lara and Gus Logie. Fair dinkum, it was like a nightmare. I felt crook in the guts. Things picked up a little when I stumbled into an adjoining bedroom and saw Mo sound asleep and sandwiched between Joel Garner and Curtly Ambrose. Poor bastard was shitting watermelons for six weeks.

The second day's play was the same-old, same-old. I carried the drinks and death-rode the side. At stumps, Malcolm Speed told us we'd have to attend an official function that night, commemorating the anniversary of the famous 1960 tied test between Australia and the West Indies.

All the old legends of the game were at this dinner. I found myself deep in conversation with Windies great Clive Lloyd, who was not only a great cricketer but, as I found out, a great bloke as well. To get our friendship off on the right note, I laced his beers with double vodkas. Let me tell you, the big fella was looking mighty shabby by the time he was due on stage to give the keynote speech. In fact, Clive had to be assisted up the stairs to the microphone, where he mumbled a few obscenities before toppling to the floor like a giant palm tree.

I wasted no time jumping on stage and shaving off the great man's eyebrows while he lay there completely out of it. Next thing, I was being attacked by the whole West Indian cricket team. I was able to keep them at bay, and even had the satisfaction of knocking out Larry Gomes before I was finally overpowered and had seven shades of shit beaten out of me.

I don't remember too much of what happened after that. All I know is that when I came to, I was tied up in the hold of a Qantas jumbo bound for home. For some reason I was never picked to play cricket for Australia again.

13

THE LEGENDARY DOUBLE

NOT A WEEK WENT by during my bush sojourn that a big-spending club didn't bang on my door trying to lure me back to the NRL competition. It was all very tempting, but I was enjoying myself far too much. After I quit the West Tamworth Robins and had my little cricket fling, I headed down south and led the Snowy River Bears to the title. I stayed with the Bears for a further season before I accepted the captain–coach job with the Junee Diesels and savoured more premiership success. Then I moved on to another town in need of my services and happy to pay handsomely for the privilege, stayed a while, and when inevitably I'd achieved glory, I moved on again to Nambucca Heads, Wagga, Dubbo, Condobolin, West Wyalong . . . and who knows where else. Things were going great for me and I enjoyed the whole experience so much that I lost my sense

'Great team. Shit city.' Holding aloft the FA Cup with Manchester United. The game was just a blur due to the excitement and the amount of piss pumping through my veins.

of time. When fans ask me how long I played in the bush, I reply, 'F**k knows!' It could have been six years, it could have 10, or 20. Country footy certainly didn't hurt my representative career. I was called up to the New South Wales State of Origin side on a few occasions and it was only vicious interstate politics that kept me out of the Australian team.

I must admit, though, that despite all my success in the bush, from time to time I got itchy feet about relaunching my big league career. Just when I was tossing up whether I'd rejoin the Knights, or become a Rooster, an Eel, a Shark or a Dragon, out of nowhere came a late-night call from Maurice Lindsay, chairman of the mighty English club team, Wigan. Maurice wanted me to join the cherry and whites, and made me an offer I couldn't refuse.

Apart from the entire country being full of poms, I liked England. A few years back I'd had a fine year with the Manchester Meerkats in the Aussie off-season. My feats on the field made me the club's hero, but the experience did end on a bit of a sour note when its president accused me of screwing his daughter. I was horrified. I did screw his wife and mother, but *never* his daughter.

Nonetheless, Manchester was a good experience for me, so when Maurice offered me a playing position at Wigan I jumped at the chance. I assured Ruthie and the kids that England was no place for a young family. The pommy weather was too harsh and the pubs too smoky, and the last thing I wanted was for the kids to come home with asthma. So, while my tribe remained in sunny Nambucca, I headed for Sydney airport to catch a jumbo to the old mother country.

I checked in at the Qantas counter and was pleasantly surprised to be served by an old flame. She was a top bird and we'd been inseparable for a while there, until I got sick of it all and slapped an AVO order on her. She wanted to cuddle after sex and all that.

Anyway, we chatted, agreed to let bygones be bygones, and, God bless her, she upgraded me to business class. That was another world. The seats were roomier, the food actually tasted like food and the grog was a revelation. I drank bucketloads of Moët and Grange, and entertained the whole section with my impersonations of Hollywood stars and by singing various Rugby League songs. By the time we reached Hong Kong, the whole plane was singing, 'When the West Tamworth Robins go bob-bob-bobbin' along . . .'

Jesus, is there nowhere I can go without becoming a cult hero?

At Hong Kong we had a night's stopover. The first thing that struck me about the place was the smell. Fair dinkum, it was like the whole city had stepped in dogshit. I didn't want to be a whinger so I stuck a couple of earplugs up my nostrils and headed out to savour the culture. I couldn't believe how many Asians there were in Hong Kong. It was just like the Gold Coast, and what made it worse was that most of the stupid bastards couldn't speak English.

I decided to do a spot of shopping, and let's just say Reggie cut a swathe through the island's jewellery stores. These blokes had no idea. Would you believe I haggled one naïve jeweller down to the point that he sold me a Rolex for $50, and then I bought Ruthie a pearl necklace for $25! It was amazing. Unfortunately, the Rolex never worked (lucky I already had one), but 12 months later I sold it to Father

Brian, our virtually blind parish priest, for a thousand bucks. Just another Reg Reagan feel-good story.

Soon it was time to board the plane again. I took my seat, ordered a beer, a red wine and a glass of Moselle, and settled in for the second leg of the journey. Sitting next to me was a nice Scottish fellow. At first I thought he was a bit surly but after a few drinks he loosened right up. We chatted cordially for a while until we moved onto the subject of sport, and then our conversation really took off. I decided to put modesty aside and must have rattled on for three hours about my Rugby League stardom and many other sporting achievements. I could tell the Scotsman was intrigued.

After I drew breath, he said he'd like to tell me about his life. I took a sleeping tablet and told him he had exactly 15 minutes.

When this bloke introduced himself I thought his name sounded familiar, but it wasn't until he started gasbagging about 'his' Manchester United that it clicked he was Sir Alex Ferguson, possibly soccer's greatest manager and the kingpin of the great Man U. Sir Alex waffled on for five or six minutes but as he started to big-note about his knighthood, I fell asleep.

I had a solid five-hour kip. When I awoke, Sir Alex grilled me about how I kept up my high playing standards and my dedication to training year after year. I could see he was scheming something but I didn't know exactly what. Our encounter obviously made a huge impression on him because he wrote about it in his top-selling autobiography, *Tartan Balls*:

> *I was having a bit of trouble at Manchester United. Blackburn had pipped us for the title and although we*

The Legendary Double

had Eric Cantona coming back from his long suspension, there was no guarantee he would be the same player. I tried to buy a few guys on the transfer market but was unsuccessful. I was worried. I knew my young squad needed a little something special. It's not easy to teach youngsters about mental toughness and ruthlessness. You need someone out on the field showing them how to do it. I didn't have that key man.

Then, in a strange twist of fate, on a flight from Hong Kong to Manchester I found myself sitting next to an Australian laddie sporting a beer gut and a moustache as big as a sporran. My first impression of him was that he had an alcohol problem and the worst body odour I'd ever sucked up my nostrils. Turned out he was on his way to play Rugby League for Wigan. We talked or, more to the point, he *talked. It was all about himself, and I must say I was deeply impressed by the guy. He had an energy and intensity. Sure, he was crass and crude, but I liked the way he wasn't intimidated by what others thought. I started pondering that maybe, just maybe, he might be the person to put steel into my talented young team. Reg was telling me how he was known far and wide for always being a man of his word, when I cut in and asked him what was the chance of him getting out of his Wigan contract. He said, 'No worries . . . nothing's been signed.'*

I then asked him if he was interested in joining Manchester United. He sat stony-faced, took a thoughtful swig of his Moselle, and said, 'F**kin' oath!'

Sir Alex was keen to know whether I'd ever played soccer. I told him that although I believed it was essentially a game

THIS IS MY LIFE!

played by faggots, I had been an outstanding junior player and had actually taken part in two senior games for Newcastle KB United. I was so good a young player that I'd been offered a trial with Nottingham Forest, but turned it down to concentrate on Rugby League. I added that although I hadn't played soccer at a competitive level for a couple of decades, my occasional kickabouts with the kids in the park left me in no doubt that I'd lost absolutely nothing.

When I arrived at Manchester airport, Maurice Lindsay was waiting for me with 100 or more Wigan supporters waving, chanting and throwing streamers. It sure took the wind out of their balloons when I marched right past them without a word and climbed into a limo with Sir Alex. We were off to Old Trafford.

The next day Sir Alex and the Manchester United chairman, Martin Edwards, held a press conference to announce my signing. As I was paraded in front of them, the journos and cameramen sat there expressionless. Amazing as it sounds, they had no idea who I was. Some shook their heads and chuckled. I made a mental note that by season's end they'd be eating kilos of my shit.

One columnist asked me what I thought of Manchester. Honesty is always the best policy, so I told him their city reminded me of my dear old aunt: cold, ugly and stinking of smoke. Well, didn't the tabloids have some fun with that. They called me everything from a beer-guzzling, ungrateful yobbo to an acid-tongued, sleazy, smelly, alcoholic descendant of a convict. To be truthful I'd heard this many times before, and simply laughed it off.

My first day at training with Man U was an experience, with all these bloody wogball pretty boys turning up in their

The Legendary Double

sports cars, expensive suits and thousand-quid haircuts. By riding a pushbike to the ground I made a point of showing I was a man of the people who was always keeping fit. I have to say, it was hard going pedalling through a metre of snow. By the time I reached Old Trafford, I had frostbite. I was used to tropical Nambucca Heads and learned a useful lesson that first day: wearing a singlet and Speedos is a no-no in northern England.

Sir Alex introduced me to all the boys. Their greeting was a touch frosty, but it didn't take me long to get the necessary respect. We were doing skills work and while all these blokes were pretty good with their feet, I was excellent with my elbows. Poofs like this young bloke named Beckham blew up as I laid into them, but Sir Alex, a Glasgow lad, enjoyed my strong-arm tactics immensely.

I became good mates with two of the United players, Roy Keane and Eric Cantona, who'd been booted out of the game for a period for karate-kicking a heckler in the crowd. Roy and Eric were very much in the mould of my old buddies Tommy Raudonikis and Les Boyd, and we were kindred spirits. After training, they'd pick me up at my joint and we'd spend the night at the pub drinking copious amounts of piss and looking for a reason to punch the shit out of any bloke who walked through the door.

The season began magnificently for us, and I was patrolling the midfield with skill, vision and thuggery. After a big win over our rivals, Liverpool, their ace striker Robbie Fowler came out in the press and called for me to be banned from the game. He accused me of sticking my fingers in his eyes, punching him in the back of the head repeatedly, kicking him in the balls . . . oh, and he also reckoned I bit him on the penis.

THIS IS MY LIFE!

I didn't deny any of this. You see, where I come from, the biff goes hand in hand with victory. In my Wests days, if I'd come off the field and hadn't been punched, gouged and squirrel-gripped at least a dozen times, I'd have lodged an official complaint.

Thanks mainly to me, Man U were riding high on the table, six points clear of the next best team. 'Love Reagan or hate him, he's the key signing of the summer,' raved the *Daily Mirror*.

In a big game against Blackburn, we were behind 2–0 with 15 minutes to go. With Sir Alex screaming from the sideline in desperation, I knew it was time to step up and really earn the hundreds of pounds I was being paid. I went on a rampage. I set up a goal for Cantona with a classy back-heel, then blasted home two goals in injury time to snatch victory. The Old Trafford faithful loved me. Yet again, I found myself a hero.

My purple patch of good form continued in the following four matches, as we notched wins over Southampton, Aston Villa, Arsenal and Leeds. Against Leeds, I scored a late goal to put us ahead 1–0, and even the notoriously one-sided Leeds fans applauded me wildly. But that didn't last, for minutes later I innocently mistook their goalie's head for the ball. I was red-carded to the hoots of the Leeds mob, but silenced them gloriously when I gave their manager, Howard Wilkinson, a sly little dry root as I passed him on my way to the sheds. Wilkinson, the sour-faced prick, blew up at the press conference after the game and accused me of trying to buggerise him. I hit back brilliantly by humming the Kylie Minogue hit 'I Should Be So Lucky'.

I copped a two-week suspension but that didn't bother

The Legendary Double

me, for I was finding the sodden English grounds heavy going and needed to freshen myself up. Manchester is a gloomy, drab-looking place, but appearances can deceive. The city has sensational nightlife and the music scene rocks.

When I was 13, I was in a band called The Bleach Boys. We played birthday parties, fetes, and other functions around Cessnock. We were pretty hot and even scored a recording contract. We would have been as big as Kids in the Kitchen, but our bass guitarist and drummer got caught up in the drug scene, and then we all grew apart. Yet, I've never got music out of my blood, and all my life I've enjoyed strumming away and knocking 'em dead at karaoke nights and campfire sing-alongs. Such is my vocal range that some have described my voice as a cross between Anne Murray and Johnny Rotten. To this very day, my guitar playing reminds people of Liberace.

The Manchester music scene allowed me to become a rock 'n' roll animal again. I was often seen chilling out at various gigs with my close friends Noel and Liam Gallagher, Mick Hucknall, and the boys from Blur. Sir Alex Ferguson was very understanding and allowed me plenty of freedom to follow my passion for music.

One night after I'd belted out a few tunes at Manchester's coolest nightclub, Noel Gallagher told me I was wasting my talent by devoting myself to sport. His words got me thinking. Hey, here I was in one of the world's great music cities, with a superstar following; I had a strong fan base because of all the goals I'd banged in for Man U. Surely this was the perfect time to launch a career in rock 'n' roll.

Noel helped me assemble a group of young, keen musos who could learn from me and complement my style.

Naturally, I was lead vocalist and played lead guitar. We practised in an abandoned warehouse owned by Sir Alex and, without getting too carried away, we were f**kin' cookin'.

Although some of the guys thought that my voice didn't suit the band and I'd be better off playing an instrument like the bongos or the triangle, I told them, as I jammed a drumstick up the arse of our 'talented' bass player, that as far as I was concerned it was my band and I'd do as I liked. Wisely, they reversed their opinions.

I balanced my band and Man U commitments beautifully by turning up to soccer training whenever I felt like it. For a short time, Sir Alex was a bit concerned that my lack of footy practice would affect the team's performance, but I put his fears at rest when I starred in our next two big wins, over Newcastle and Everton.

In some quarters I was being called the new George Best. Like George, I was a super sportsman, an alcoholic and a champion womaniser. I'm proud to say, however, that I resisted the sheilas' charms and fended them off to less charismatic, uglier teammates, like David Beckham. This is exactly how Becks hooked up with Posh Spice.

After just a month's jamming, the band started playing a few gigs around Manchester and we won rave reviews from the city's hard-to-please music writers. By the time we did our fourth concert, we were selling out 2000-seat venues. We were calling ourselves Freekick to cash in on my soccer fame, but I thought it sounded corny and I called a meeting of the band to choose a new name. We needed something strong, one that would stand out and show what we were all about. I came up with The Reg Reagan Band and after six hours' discussion, the boys reluctantly agreed.

The Legendary Double

Meanwhile, back at Old Trafford, Manchester United was killing 'em in the premiership and we were also making our way nicely through the FA Cup. We had a tough Cup quarterfinal against Sunderland and got through thanks to Paul Scholes's late strike. In the semifinal of this world famous comp we drew Arsenal, who were fast becoming our main rival.

It wasn't easy playing a gig and partying till five, then getting out of bed at six to meet my soccer commitments, but I was doing it in fine style and both the band and Man U were really going places. Leading up to the semi against Arsenal, the boys and I really trained our backsides off. As I sat on the sideline on a banana chair sipping a cocktail, I commented to Sir Alex, as he rubbed suntan lotion into my shoulders, that I was so proud of the players' professionalism. Sir Alex leaned forward and whispered into my ear, 'Reg, I am so proud of you.' His words gave me a strange feeling of pride and homophobia.

The Reg Reagan Band got some huge news days before the Arsenal game. We were to play Manchester Arena, which has a capacity of 12,000 people. The timing was perfect because we'd just released our first single, 'Born with a Silver Spoon in Your Rectum', and it was roaring up the charts. We were definitely bound for stardom, but we didn't kid ourselves, we knew we had some fine-tuning to do.

We were invited onto TV's *Top of the Pops* to perform our single, and I thought it would be a good idea to smash our instruments at the end of the song, in that great rock 'n' roll tradition. The Man U boys popped into the television station to be part of the studio audience. Unhappily, things got ugly when, right in the middle of my guitar-smashing frenzy,

THIS IS MY LIFE!

I accidentally clocked our star winger, Ryan Giggs, and fractured his cheekbone. This ruled Giggsy out of the semifinal, so I felt a great responsibility to put in a big game against Arsenal.

That match was an epic. It went into extra time, with the scores locked at 1–1. I was being heavily marked by Lee Dixon and Martin Keown, and for 100 minutes their double-teaming, and the massive hangover I was suffering after getting on the piss the night before, was doing the trick and keeping me quiet. Then, an inspired moment! Gary Neville delivered a long ball up to Eric Cantona, who floated out to the left. I supported him and we played a delicate one–two manoeuvre, which put the Frenchman into space with only Arsenal goalie David Seaman to beat. Eric feigned to shoot one way, and tried to chip over Seaman's head and into the net, but the goalie read it beautifully and punched the ball away. Unfortunately for his team, he punched it in my direction. I jostled for space with Dixon and Keown and then, in one fluid movement, hit the ball on the volley and watched with delight as it sailed into the top corner of the net. The stadium exploded. We were in the FA Cup Final.

In the sheds straight after, Sir Alex told us to stay focused. If we won the next two premiership games, the league title was ours and then we could think about the legendary double: the premiership and the FA Cup.

Just when it seemed that life could get no better, it suddenly did. I learned on the bus taking us home to Manchester that my band's single was No. 1 throughout Britain. Topping the charts made us a big national act and on the eve of our follow-up single, 'Cross-Dressing Window Cleaner', we played some major venues down in London.

The Legendary Double

At the same time, Man U thrashed Leicester City 6–0 and we only had to beat Tottenham Hotspur at home to be Premier League champions. In the lead-up to the Spurs game, we had some injury concerns. Roy was suffering a knee complaint, Eric had a groin strain, Nicky Butt had rolled his ankle, and David Beckham had a bad hair day. Sir Alex wisely rested these guys, because he was confident of beating Tottenham without them and the FA Cup Final was looming. I was selected as striker against Spurs, the first time I'd ever played up-front.

The Tottenham section of the crowd, sensing I had the key to the match, really gave me a hard time, singing in unison for the entire first half, 'Reggie's a poofter . . . ' I won them over, though, by coming on in the second half wearing a black leather miniskirt. Who says I take myself too seriously?

Tottenham put big Sol Campbell on me, but my vision and movement were too much for him. We blew Spurs out of the water with high-tempo soccer. We won 4–1 and the debut striker, yours truly, scored a hat trick.

We were crowned league champions and did a lap of honour at Old Trafford. As a tribute to Man U's favourite Australian, the PA system played one of The Reg Reagan Band's songs, '26-inch Love Thruster'. The place went crazy. Even Sir Alex had his shirt off, banging his head to my guitar solo.

We celebrated that night, and in the morning had a team meeting where the manager stressed that with only two weeks before the FA Cup Final, it was imperative that we work harder than ever at training. I backed him up before pissing off early to band practice.

THIS IS MY LIFE!

'Cross-Dressing Window Cleaner' had followed 'Born with a Silver Spoon in Your Rectum' to the top of the charts, and '26-inch Love Thruster' was sitting nicely at No. 5. We were in enormous demand. Then came news that blew our minds. Our agent interrupted a jam session, and he was so excited he could hardly get the words out. Finally, he drew breath and blurted, 'We're booked to play Wembley!' Only four months before, we'd been jamming in Sir Alex's warehouse. I nearly fainted with excitement. In two weeks, I'd be dancing on Wembley's hallowed turf with a soccer ball at my feet. Now I was in line to play my guitar and sing at the fabled field of dreams.

There was just one small problem. The gig was on 20 July. The game was on 21 July. I rang Sir Alex to tell him I'd be doing the Wembley double, but far from saying 'congratulations' he tore shreds off me. He screamed down the line that if I played with the band on the Friday, I'd be warming the bench on Saturday. In a panic, I called our agent to see if there was any chance of pushing the gig back, but he said that was impossible. In fact, the day after the Cup Final, the developers were due to start tearing Wembley down for renovation.

There was nothing to do but go on the front foot with Sir Alex. 'Listen, you dirty Scottish haggis! I'm playing the f**kin' gig and if you bench me it'll be on your bald head when Liverpool kick our arse!' Sir Alex backed right down. He was bluffing, and being a bully myself I know how to treat blokes like him. He quietly expressed his concern that the concert would leave me tired and leg-weary, and he did have a point. In their semi, Liverpool had blown Newcastle off the park with their high-tempo game and the

The Legendary Double

Merseysiders were playing with a mile of confidence. I told Sir Alex that I'd tone down my on-stage antics. He took things just a bit too far when he asked me to lay off the grog as well. We struck a compromise and I promised Sir Alex I'd be in bed by 4 am.

Sir Alex remained a bit cool on the idea of me performing at Wembley on the eve of the Cup Final, but my Manchester United teammates were ecstatic, and I got them tickets for the big show. We – or, rather, they – trained brilliantly going into the final. I chose to rest my legs and vocal cords, and spent most of the week propping up the Old Trafford bar, drinking myself into a winning frame of mind.

When I wasn't boozing I was with the band. We came up with a few new songs for Wembley and I even made a new backdrop for the stage. The boys thought it was a bit too much, but I reckoned it was brilliant the way I'd depicted myself as Jesus Christ sitting at the Last Supper surrounded by my Manchester United teammates, who were the apostles; meaning followers; meaning not as good.

The city of Manchester was abuzz with almost the entire population of the city attending either the concert, the Cup Final, or, like me, both. The day before the gig I drove down to London to prepare. I'd made a date to meet the Man U boys on the morning of the game. I did countless radio and TV interviews. They all asked the same question: how did it feel to have pulled off this amazing double?

I appeared on *Parkinson*, which was going well until Michael broke the news that he was a Liverpool supporter. I couldn't believe the grey-haired old weasel could be so rude as to invite me on, then insult me like that. BBC TV banned me from ever again coming within 50 metres of their studios after I gave the beloved host a broken nose, cheekbone, jaw, and, for good measure, showed him first-hand how I was going to score the winning goal against his precious Liverpool. This particular demonstration left his scrotum resembling an elephant's beanbag.

On the morning of the gig I woke in my suite at the Dorchester Hotel on Park Lane all revved up. This was the beginning of what looked like being my finest 36 hours. I met up with the band in one of the guy's rooms and just as we were halfway through trashing it, our manager phoned to tell us the Wembley concert was a sell-out. We high-fived, hugged and smashed lamps over each other's heads in anticipation of playing in front of a huge crowd.

We caught the bus to Wembley at 5 pm. The streets were lined with fans cheering and waving banners, scarves and posters. My band was a little nervous. Unlike me, these blokes weren't used to a big occasion. I reassured them: 'We've done the work, we have the talent. All that's left to do is *rock 'n' roll!*'

I'd had some slabs of KB especially imported for the gig; backstage I was throwing them down like it was my 21st and I had a nice little shine up. I glanced out to the huge stadium and could see it was filling up quickly. The crowd was really giving our support act a hard time. They were throwing cans, bottles and abuse at these poor buggers, until finally Bono and the boys said, 'F**k it!' and cleared the way for The Reg Reagan Band's grand appearance.

We huddled backstage, keeping our energy tight. The chanting of 100,000 people let us know that they were not about to settle for anything less than our very, very best. And that's what we were going to give them.

The Legendary Double

I peeked at the crowd from behind the amplifiers. I got the shock of my life to see oceans upon oceans of people. It made me a bit nervous. Then, to my surprise, I saw Sir Alex Ferguson in the front row. He was shirtless again and 'I Love Rockin' Reggie' was painted on his chest. F**kin' hell, two days before he wouldn't talk to me, but give him a free ticket and the tight Scottish prick becomes a groupie.

I marched back to the band and gave them a quick team talk. Then we lifted our German beer mugs high and toasted the Gods of Rock 'n' Roll. 'Let's do it!' I screamed and we ran on stage to a roar so loud that it nearly collapsed the old twin towers of Wembley. Without missing a beat, we launched into our fourth single, 'Sperm Bank Robbery'. We were nervous but didn't show it. The rum we were knocking back from our water bottles might have helped.

I kept my promise to Sir Alex that I'd preserve my energy, and didn't run around the stage like a maniac. Instead, I fell back on some subtle stagecraft to get the crowd going. The fans lost control completely when I poured hot wax on my genitals and walked on my hands across burning coals. Wembley was in a state of hysteria as we lived up to our billing as the best live rock band in Britain. After our closing number, 'Retirement Village Pervert', we thanked the crowd and walked off-stage.

We sat in our dressing room enjoying a beer or two, while the crowd screamed for an encore. Of course we obliged, and charged out and gave 'em the old ACDC favourite, 'Whole Lotta Rosie'. We finished off with a couple of our own hits, then, as we were about to walk off, I led the fans in a rousing rendition of 'Glory, Glory, Man United', as a little rev-up to my teammates for tomorrow.

I slumped in my chair backstage drenched in sweat, exhausted but still running on adrenalin. The enormity of my achievement hit me. I was so pumped I felt like going out there and doing it all again. But instead, I relaxed with a cold KB and the strains of the crowd singing in unison, 'There's Only One Reggie Reagan'. I don't know if it was the rum, the dozen KBs or the bottle of scotch I drank throughout the gig, but I was high on life!

I looked at my watch. It was midnight. You beaut! I'd promised my tight-arsed manager, Sir Alex, I'd be in the sack by 4 am, and there were still four hours to go. A limo whisked the band and me to a private club in London to celebrate. The club was jumping. It was all great fun, so I drank up, smoked like a chimney, and danced with every ugly sheila in the place, till I reckoned it was about 4 am, home-time. As I left the club, I was amazed to see the sun was up. I'd lost track of time and actually it was a little later than four. In fact, it was nine-thirty.

I called Sir Alex on my mobile, and told him I'd slept well and was raring to go. He thanked me for my professionalism and told me to be in the Wembley sheds at one-thirty. Shit! What should I do? Go back to the Dorchester and jam in three hours' sleep? No, that was pointless, all it would do was give my hangover a chance to get me in its grip. So, I did the only sensible thing. I strolled into the nearest pub and continued drinking.

There I sat in a deserted little bar in East London, throwing beers back and listening to Supertramp, Deep Purple and Motorhead on the jukebox. I booked a cab to pick me up at midday to ensure I got to the stadium on time, then I chatted to the barkeep for an hour or so. By eleven-thirty I was

The Legendary Double

getting pretty bloody tired. This was the sign to move on to the harder stuff and I polished off a nice big bottle of vodka. By the time the taxi arrived, the barkeep had to carry me out and throw me into the back seat. I wasn't worried, however, because, being an elite sportsman, I knew my recovery time and that I'd be at my peak and ready to go by the two-thirty kickoff.

The cab ride was torture. I had to tell the driver to pull over four or five times so I could spew into the gutter. I guess I must have been car sick or had a dose of food poisoning. Eventually, we reached Wembley. Manchester United fans would have felt pessimistic about their team's chances when they saw a green Reg Reagan fall out of his taxi at 1.45 pm, hugging a half-empty bottle of vodka.

I walked into the dressing room, and the boys and Sir Alex ran up to me. They showed that same mixture of relief and respect as Potsie and the guys would display when Fonzie rocked into Arnold's. Then Sir Alex sniffed the air. 'Christ almighty, Reggie, I'm getting pissed just standing next to you!'

I assured him I was OK. 'Just get me my jumper, polish my boots and smother me in Dencorub, and I'll destroy these Liverpool bastards,' I slurred, with the arrogance only alcohol can induce.

The warm-up was a bloody nightmare. The ball looked about as big as a split pea and I was badly dehydrated. I told one of the trainers that throughout the match he had to make sure my water bottle was full of vodka and that every time there was a stoppage, to bring it out to me. After Sir Alex's pre-game talk, during which I fell asleep and pissed my pants, it was time to line up and take the slow walk onto the pitch.

In the tunnel I found myself standing beside Liverpool defender Steve McManaman. 'Christ, Reg, you look terrible. What have you been up to?' he asked with a smartarse smirk.

'Screwing your old man, he sends his regards,' was my brilliant retort.

We lined up on the pitch to be introduced to Queen Elizabeth, who passed along the Man U and Liverpool lines shaking hands and making small talk. A little drama occurred after I 'allegedly' grabbed Her Majesty's breast. Truth be known, it was all a case of mistaken identity. I *did* go the grope, but I was so pissed I thought she was Britney Spears.

Anyway, after they played the wanky pommy national anthem, it was game on. We started slowly. Liverpool slotted right into their passing game, which starved us of possession. The pace of the match and the unseasonal hot weather was making life a bit tough for old Reggie, but I'd played in difficult conditions a million times before and knew how to pace myself.

Suddenly Robbie Fowler headed in a goal off a corner to send Liverpool ahead 1–0, and our quest for the great double was looking shaky. At half-time I could sense panic among our guys. I awoke from my slumber on the rubbing bench to reassure the boys that all was going to be OK, then I dozed off again.

Unfortunately, at the beginning of the second half we were playing no better than in the first. We were still struggling for consistent possession. Then we found ourselves in deep trouble when Liverpool's John Barnes scored from a free kick just outside the box to put us 2–0 in arrears. I looked to

The Legendary Double

the touchline and Sir Alex was shitting bricks. Then I looked at the clock and there was only 20 minutes left. It was time for 'The White Pele', as I had come to be known, to take charge.

I stopped pissing around on the flanks and pushed upfront a little further. Roy Keane started to win the battle of the midfield, and began supplying me with lots of quality ball. I took advantage of these chances straight away. Roy knocked the ball up at my feet and I could feel my marker Neil Ruddock's breath on the back of my neck. To lose him, I performed a delicate little backheel right through his legs, spun around and accelerated swiftly past. Their goalkeeper, David James, rushed off his line towards me but I wrong-footed him with a swivel of my hips. Then I coolly slotted the ball into the back of the Liverpool net. The crowd roared, and I pulled my jumper up over my head, revealing my manly torso, and ran to them, sliding on my knees across the Wembley turf up to the perimeter fence. My joyous teammates piled on top of me. Fifteen minutes to go and we were back in the match with a fighting chance.

But Liverpool made us work. Instead of folding, they pressed hard for the next eight minutes, launching raid after raid on our goal line. With six minutes remaining in the game, Robbie Fowler drilled a low shot at our goal. From where I stood, it looked in, and only a miracle save by our goalie, Peter Schmeichel, kept it out. Pete didn't waste a second. He sprang to his feet and threw the ball my way. From being under siege we were now on the counterattack, with space to move.

I dribbled my way upfield, weaving through the dumbfounded defenders. Then I saw Eric Cantona looming on my left. I held onto the ball for a second to give Eric the opportunity to shake off his marker. I then laid on a pinpoint accurate pass to the Frenchman, who rammed home a beauty. It was all locked up at 2–2. Wembley was roaring, just like it had been 16 hours earlier, and both times it was because of yours truly.

Both sides went on to the attack and played with incredible intensity through injury time until the final whistle. It was Golden Goal time. We'd play 10 minutes' extra each way and the first team to score was the winner. Five minutes into extra time, I got a terrific opportunity. As Liverpool fumbled around in defence, I intercepted a pass and from 20 metres out, booted a stinging shot that looked to be in all the way – until it rebounded off the crossbar. I couldn't believe it. 'Maybe I *am* human!' I screamed in frustration. Both sides had more chances, but at the end of the 20 minutes the scores remained at 2–2.

The FA Cup Final would be decided by a penalty shoot-out. Liverpool had their five guys ready, and they lined up for their shots, but Sir Alex was still tossing up who would do the job for Manchester United. I was the logical No. 1 choice, but was suffering cramp in every part of my anatomy. I could hardly walk, but insisted on playing my part. Eric was first up for us and whacked the ball in for 1–0. Liverpool's turn, and Phil Babb nervously beat Schmeichel to make it 1–1 in the big shoot-out. Now Roy Keane took position. The Irishman jigged up to the ball and hit it well. 2–1. Next up strutted Fowler. The Fowl hit the ball with enormous power but Pete saved wonderfully. The score remained at 2–1, and all we had to do was hold our nerve and pot the next goal to win. Our defender, Denis Irwin,

The Legendary Double

stepped up and did a Fowler. He kicked the ball clear over the crossbar. Liverpool's Steve McManaman showed his skill by equalising 2–2. Both teams had two kicks left. Our Gary Pallister, a man of great experience, didn't let us down: Manchester 3–2. Then Liverpool's John Barnes choked and pushed the ball past the left-hand post. Still 3–2 to us. This was it. If we scored with our next kick, the FA Cup was bound for Old Trafford and we would be winners of English soccer's mighty double.

Sir Alex was frantic. He needed a man with ice in his veins to score this high-pressure goal. Wembley held its breath. I leapt from the stretcher where the doctor had been working on my cramps and yelled, 'Give it here, Fergie!' Sir Alex gave me the ball. The cheer could be heard miles away. Fifty thousand red scarves, beanies and G-strings flew high into the air. I shot a wry grin at David James, who I could see was a bundle of nerves. Me, I was still well under the influence of alcohol and feeling no pressure. I put the ball on the mark and had a little dry retch. The stadium hushed. The ref blew his whistle. I moved back a few paces then surged onto the ball, my head down. I was about to unleash pure fury on it when I looked up and saw James. He'd lost his nerve and prematurely dived to his left. I smiled to myself and slotted the ball in the opposite direction. GOOAAAAALLLLLLL!!!

Fans and teammates fought to be the ones to hoist me onto their shoulders and carry me high. The hysteria lasted for what seemed an hour until we had to do the Wembley walk and make our way up the stairs to be presented with the FA Cup. Our captain, Eric Cantona, held the trophy aloft. I stood next to him, exhausted, emotionally drained and hungover. For good measure, I received the BBC's Man of the Match award. What an unbelievable day and a half it had been for me.

As I walked off the pitch and plonked myself into the hot tub with my uncircumcised English teammates, two things crossed my mind. The first was that life just could not get any better than this. The second was that there was no way our communal bath would meet health regulations.

I'd reached the top of the tree in rock 'n' roll *and* soccer. Should I tempt fate and continue my glittering dual career in England, or simply walk away secure in the knowledge that I was a legend and that the name Reg Reagan would be etched forever into music and sporting history?

I chose to stay. But the British government refused to renew my working visa when Queen Elizabeth threatened to press charges over the groping incident if I wasn't deported.

What happened to the band? Well, I split up with them right after the Wembley triumph. We argued over money. These blokes believed they deserved to be paid.

I returned to my beloved Australia. The British Airways jet I flew home on had a huge picture of old Reggie on the side, as a tribute to all my achievements in England. Pity those tight pommy arseholes wouldn't upgrade me to business class. But I didn't care. As the plane neared the end of its flight, I looked down upon Sydney Harbour and knew there would be many other highs awaiting me.

14

RUGBY LEAGUE WARRIOR

MY LITTLE CRICKETING ADVENTURE had certainly helped raise the Reagan profile in Pakistan, India and Trinidad. It had also helped me score sponsorship deals with major companies on the Subcontinent and opened the door to me becoming great mates with a bookmaker named John. It served another very useful purpose: giving me much-needed time out of the Rugby League spotlight.

The months away from my first sporting love freshened me up and revamped my intense passion for the game. However, Rugby League had changed since I'd left it. The Super League War had broken out between a new entity owned by Rupert Murdoch's News Limited and the establishment Australian Rugby League. Naturally, when news broke that I was coming back to the code, both sides started an all-out assault to get my signature.

'See you in court, Pretty Boy…' I wonder who Jonny Wilkinson stole his trademark kicking style off?'

Of course, I wasn't the only player the ARL and Super League were fighting over – just the best – and plenty of the other guys started calling around at my house to get my advice on who to sign with. I took full advantage of their confusion and naivety, and volunteered to manage them for a mere 25 per cent of their sign-on fees. It was deeply satisfying to be able to help all these other players out, and having about 30 blokes on my books also gave me a fair slab of power when negotiating my own contract.

At times I felt a bit guilty about taking my fellow players' money, but it must be pointed out that these blokes got great service for their 25 per cent. Each one received a carton of beer, which I stuck around to drink with them. They got an autographed photo of yours truly, and any time they went away for a weekend or an extended period, I would house-sit for them. Their wives and girlfriends received a free 'Thai' massage from me every fortnight, and if the boys' sex lives started to get a bit rocky, I'd be there to counsel them or give a practical demonstration with their loved one of how to get things back on track. And, of course, I advised the boys on the right way to spend their newfound wealth.

Lots of big-time wankers in power suits make their clients invest in real estate or the share market. But I found these avenues overrated and really f**king boring to boot. No, my players put their money into Jet Skis, sports cars and ostrich farms.

To this day, if you speak to any of the guys, most of whom, incidentally, you'll now find sleeping in doorways in Kings Cross, they speak of me in absolutely glowing terms. In fact, whenever I run into them, they throw themselves at my feet and bow . . . or beg for food. How's that for gratitude!

Anyway, back in the footy war, after a week or so, I had all my players signed and ready to ply their trade with the elite clubs of the game: Adelaide, Paris Saint-Germain, Gold Coast or Gateshead Thunder. Then it was my turn, and the media was having a field day speculating on who'd win my signature: the ARL or Super League.

Money wasn't the main issue. Shit, I was making enough sponging off all my clients. What I wanted was to play in a competition that would give me the profile I deserved. While Super League promised to make me a household name in Libya, Afghanistan and Greenland, the ARL promised to make me their top player and raise my profile to the exalted level of that of a prime minister or Sydney Cricket Ground streaker.

It was difficult – I had great mates on both sides of the war. I respected Super League's vision of spreading the game all over the planet, but felt a great loyalty to the ARL. I eventually called a major press conference to announce my decision. There was only one honourable thing to do. I signed with both of them.

Sure, the money was great, but money's like herpes, it comes and goes. No, for me, signing with both sides was all about the game's greatest player saving the sport. I would act as a bridge between the warring parties, be a bloke both the ARL's Ken 'Arko' Arthurson and Super League's John Ribot could confide in, and be a person groupies looked to for comfort in confusing times.

Unbelievably, I copped my share of criticism. Some people even called me selfish and greedy. Those critics made me want to puke in my new marble toilet.

While Rugby League copped a battering, my popularity soared. I was a martyr for the good of the game. No matter where you went, my handsome face was on a billboard, promoting either the ARL or Super League.

In one commercial for the News Limited mob, I ran shirtless along a beach to the strains of 'We Are The Champions'. Meanwhile, the ARL ads featured me singing their anthem, 'Stick It Up Your Arse, Mr Murdoch!'. It was all great fun, but, in the end, the court ruled Super League clubs had to play in the ARL comp.

This came as a great relief to me. Not only was I allowed to keep all my dough, but the ruling saved me a hell of a lot of travelling, because I'd signed with both the Brisbane Broncos and the Gold Coast Chargers. In the end, I became a Charger, because the Broncos had some weasel named Langer playing for them and coach Wayne Bennett couldn't promise me the captaincy.

I loved the Gold Coast and its unique holiday atmosphere where nothing is taken too seriously. After speaking to a few senior players I knew the football club was run exactly the same way. I was sold.

I really enjoyed the year. We played some fantastic football and were unlucky to miss out on the finals. The people on the Gold Coast fell in love with me. My teammates were totally in awe of me, too.

Then, at the end of the season, problems arose. Super League won their appeal and the court ruled that the following year they could run their own separate comp. I called a head-to-head meeting with Arko and Ribot, and, while punching the crap out of each other, they made it clear I had to play in both competitions.

I thought about this long and hard, and decided that their demand was totally out of the question. You only have one body and with the rigours of the modern game, starring in two teams at once would have killed me. Or at least the bonding sessions would have. So we compromised. The following season I'd play for the ARL, and the one after I'd turn out in the Super League.

The ARL begged me to leave the Gold Coast and join the struggling South Queensland Crushers, who would be trying to win fans away from Super League's powerhouse, Brisbane Broncos. I love a challenge, and signed on the dotted line.

The Crushers were an interesting club. They lacked the tight companionship of the Gold Coast but leading in to Christmas I really revved the boys up, and they responded to my charisma and unsurpassed knowledge of the game. I had a tremendous feeling about our chances of success in the new season. We broke for Christmas and club legend Tosser Turner told the boys we all had to be back at training on 20 January.

My festive season was sorted. I went home to Cessnock for the annual Reagan Christmas reunion. It was always a great time. The Reagan women cook up a feast, while the men and children get pissed around the above-ground pool.

I kept up my training, though, and was the Crushers' ambassador down south. I told all and sundry to get right behind this champion team. They were going places and were destined to be the league's new powerhouse side. My signing had triggered plenty of support for the much-maligned South Queensland and all over Australia on each kids' Christmas wish list was a Crushers jersey with, on the back, the number 13 and the name 'Reagan'.

Imagine my surprise when I returned to training on 20 January to find no other prick had bothered to show. Now those slack bastards were showing their true colours. This was obviously the Crushers' notorious lack of commitment, which so many people had warned me about. I rang the team officials and gave them an awful spray.

I trained on alone. In the lead-up to the season the odd player only would drag himself to the oval. Not to train, just to stand around and smirk at me busting my guts. I was getting pretty f**king pessimistic about our chances, especially when just over the hill I knew my old club, the Gold Coast Chargers, would be working their arses off as a perfect unit.

To my credit, I had rarely been in better shape and posed proudly in the Brisbane *Courier-Mail* predicting that the Crushers were about to make our opponents eat shit.

The week before the season kicked off, the ARL had a huge launch at the Sydney Town Hall. The do was attended by all the players, about 5000 supporters and various dignitaries. I chatted cordially with the other guys, telling them that this was the year my Crushers would establish themselves as a major force.

The official part of the launch began, and one by one the team's captains were asked to get up on stage. Each bloke received wild applause. I slipped on my beloved Crushers jersey and waited for the call. But, to my horror, ARL chief John Quayle didn't read out the South Queensland Crushers. I was pissed off and stormed onto the stage. 'You bald bastard! You're supposed to be the boss of this schemozzle, but you forgot the No. 1 team!' I screamed.

Quayle looked puzzled. 'Sorry, Reg. Who are you playing for again?'

I was astounded. 'The South Queensland friggin' Crushers,' I roared.

Well, the crowd was in hysterics, and Quayle had tears of mirth rolling down his cheeks as he replied, 'Reg, we kicked the f**king Crushers out three months ago!'

I went numb. Suddenly all the little signs over the last eight weeks, ones I'd ignored because I was so focused – or drunk – came rushing back to me. The press conferences I'd called that no reporter or TV crew attended, the Crushers' administration offices all boarded up, no one ever at training but Tosser Turner and me (and all Tosser would do was stick his head out his car window and call me the stupidest prick he'd ever met and drive off. And I'd thought the old bastard was just using some sort of reverse psychology).

Up on stage at the Town Hall that night I felt like a horse's arse. But the darkest hour is just before the dawn and, as I slunk off in humiliation, an unlikely ally handed me a schooner and asked me to join him at the bar.

15

HOW I WON THE COMP

MY SAVIOUR WAS THE Englishman Malcolm Reilly, coach of the Newcastle Knights. I'd played against Mal once or twice, and we were kindred spirits. We were both highly skilled ball players and enjoyed breaking opponents' jaws. Mal, as brutal as he was on the field, had a very shrewd football brain, and asked me to join the Knights.

Mal knew he had a pretty good side at Newcastle, but he said the Knights probably lacked that special little something, which I had shitloads of. There were also a lot of youngsters at the club, and he thought my experience might be invaluable to them.

To be honest, I was out of options, and I was desperate to play because I'd never been in such excellent condition. The more I thought about joining Newcastle, the more I liked it. It was an opportunity for the wife to be back close to her

'What next ... Mayor?' Thanks to me, Newcastle finally got what previous impostors always promised, a premiership.

parents in Cessnock, and a chance for me to call on a few old flames as well, if Ruthie didn't mind.

I accepted Malcolm's offer and the next day the Reagan family loaded up the old ute, chained the kids in the back and headed off down the Pacific Highway bound for Newcastle.

As we arrived in the city, a couple of Knights supporters were waving a huge banner that said, 'Newcastle Welcomes Reg, World's Greatest Footballer'. This really warmed the cockles of my heart. As we drove on, about 100 metres further, two old ladies were holding up another huge banner. This one read, 'Newcastle Welcomes Reg, World's Greatest Rooter'. I felt a familiar thumping in my pants. Ah yeah, it was great to be back.

We settled in immediately – it was just like old times. We rented a two-bedroom unit in the city, but the wife and kids spent most of their time up at Cessnock at the in-laws' house.

My first day at training was a memorable one. All the Knights boys really loved having me there and the place was abuzz. The media was all over me and lots of supporters turned up to cheer their new hero in the red and blue.

Malcolm Reilly pulled me aside early and told me that although he was coach, I should feel free to speak my mind, or pull anyone into line who I reckoned needed it. I wasted no time, and let rip into the captain, Paul Harragon. 'Chief,' as he liked to be called, was struggling to keep up with me in the fitness sessions. I told him straight: 'You're a disgrace. If you're not prepared to put in, then piss off home!'

'Get f**ked!' the Chief shot back at me. So, in front of the crowd at training, I gave the big Novocastrian an awful touch-up. The Chief had blood pouring out of every orifice. It was clear to everyone: there was a new sheriff in town.

THIS IS MY LIFE!

Mal was right about one thing. There were a lot of talented youngsters at Newcastle. One bloke in particular caught my eye, a fellow named Andrew Johns.

Johns was hanging around after training doing some kicking. I was hanging around doing some drinking. It was pretty clear the bloke didn't have a clue what he was doing, so I strode up and gave him some pointers, even showing him how to do the famous Reg Reagan banana kick. In no time he was booting the ball around like a genius. The fact that nowadays every time Johns gets up on stage to receive one of his precious little awards he neglects to mention the help I gave him, is simply water off a duck's back to me.

At that point of his career, I found Andrew Johns quite a nice young fellow. Sure, he talked a lot of shit and, going by the size of his arse, he ate a lot too, but his thirst for knowledge and beer really impressed me.

Things were great until my family got some bad news. Dad's brother, Reece, had died. Reece Reagan had been crook for quite a while and in this time I'd grown quite close to him. Uncle Reece was the black sheep of our family. He had no wife and kids, and always said that when he died I was the one he wanted to be in charge of his funeral plans. Because I was the only family member who was close to Reece, I felt a great responsibility to send him off in the right way. Problem was, I didn't know whether to have him buried or cremated. I was confused.

One thing was for sure. I looked like being up for a lot of money. The cost of a mass and then either burial or cremation was outrageous. By my reckoning I could have old Reecey stuffed and mounted for half the price ... and that's exactly what I did.

When the taxidermist dropped Uncle Reece off at my two-bedroom unit, I mounted him above the fireplace and, although he freaked out some of my visitors, I was glad to see his lifeless body hanging there each morning. Reece also had some practical uses. He doubled as a Christmas tree, and, when the boys popped around for a couple of quiet beers, he made an excellent dartboard.

As the season drew closer I felt optimistic. The Knights were a tight-knit bunch and not even my elitist attitude could change that. Strangely enough, we performed only so-so in the trials and I could feel a little panic in the camp. I immediately called a meeting and explained to the boys that we had to stay tight, forget about witch-hunts and keep the faith in our preparation.

I also told them that now was the ideal time to air any concerns or grievances, so we could address the problems and get on with our preparation for the season opener. I took it upon myself to say that I thought Paul Harragon was playing like a poof, Andrew Johns was shockingly overrated and Tony Butterfield was ready for the retirement village. I felt my honesty was appreciated by Chief and Butts, as they dragged me outside and proceeded to give me a busted kidney and three broken ribs.

But our little meeting must have done the trick, because we started the season with a bang, winning seven games in a row. As usual, my contribution was enormous. I was winding back the clock to my glory days with the West Tamworth Robins, and the Knights even offered me a two-year extension on my contract, but my goal was to focus on each year at a time so I knocked 'em back.

My season had a hiccup when I copped a knee injury.

This put me offside with my teammates. Well, not the injury so much, it was more me sitting on the hill and hurling abuse at them in the four games I missed. Fair dinkum, some blokes can't take criticism, and criticism was what they deserved, because they bloody couldn't win without me. To this day I swear that my words were well meant. I challenge anyone to tell me that 'pathetic', 'worthless', 'untalented', and 'cowardly' are anything but constructive.

Some of these little prima donnas even had the nerve to ask me to stop smoking in the sheds at halftime. The truth was I needed the marijuana for medicinal purposes. Arthritis is a real killer.

The Knights' supporters' base heaved a huge sigh of relief when I returned from my knee injury, and the side naturally started winning again. 'Winning' is an understatement. We were murdering our opponents, racking up huge scorelines, and yours truly was in sparkling touch.

Inevitably, speculation began in the press that I'd be selected for the Australian team to play the Kiwis. I took it as a compliment but, as I pointed out to the media, my rep days were over. I'd retired from representative football 10 years before, after being accused of smashing a schooner glass on a selector's head. This malicious accusation was never proven, because the selector was mysteriously run over by a Nissan Bluebird just before my trial began. I was in the clear, but the incident really sapped my passion for the rep stuff.

Anyway, I was loving my football, and football was loving me. *Rugby League Week* called me 'the competition's most influential player', and the *Newcastle Herald* described me as 'a gift to the city from the footballing gods'.

There was no end to my popularity. Everybody wanted

a piece of me. I did a few guest appearances on *Water Rats* and *Neighbours*, in which I played a peeping Tom with a fear of heights. *TV Week* proclaimed the episode 'a landmark in Australian television history'.

With only a month to go before the semis, we were sitting in second place, just behind the leaders, Manly, who were our bogey side. We were playing solid, if unspectacular, football until we put in a stinker against Parramatta away from home. Everything we touched turned to dogshit that day, and the Eels crowd delighted in heckling us as Parra put us to the sword 28–6.

I must say, some of the barracking was rather clever, particularly the insults aimed at our high and mighty halfback, Andrew Johns. Unfortunately, things got a bit out of order and way too personal when the fans directed their abuse at me. After the match I copped a life ban from Parramatta Leagues Club when I caught up with a few of the Eels' big-mouth supporters. The club management accused me of ramming their heads into a smoke machine. I found those allegations outrageous. If they'd charged me with ramming their heads into a poker machine I'd have said fair enough, but a smoke machine? Never.

That week we had a few heart-to-heart team meetings and Mal encouraged us to set personal goals for the next three weeks leading into the finals. I went home that night, had a good think about what I wanted to achieve, and this is what I wrote down:

1. Score an appearance on *Burke's Backyard*.
2. Buy a motorbike.
3. Try not to point the finger at my teammates' shortcomings.

The listing of goals was a masterstroke by Mal and we were unbeaten up to the finals.

With so many young blokes in the squad it was understandable that we were suffering a bad case of nerves going into our first semi against Parramatta. Knowing my teammates' low standards, I pointed out to them that all they had to do was give 100 per cent and that way, win, lose or draw, they could be satisfied with themselves. Personally speaking, if we bombed in the semis I knew I was going to be singling out individuals to carry the blame . . .

I was still carrying my niggling knee injury, so Mal decided to play me off the bench. I thought he was f**kin' nuts, but he was the coach, and he pointed out that our game against the Eels wasn't sudden death so it was better to wrap me in cotton wool for the crunch matches ahead.

It came as no surprise to me when, after just 20 minutes, the boys were down 18–0 and, as expected, the call came from the coach: 'Reg, you're on!'

As I strolled to the sideline to commence my high-tech warm up – put out my smoke, touch my toes three times, and holler, 'Let's kill these dirty bludgers!' – the crowd spotted me and began to chant, 'Champ-ion!, Champ-ion!' I bristled with pride and purpose. It was game on.

I didn't waste time. 'Give me the friggin' pigskin!' I screamed, and took control of the match. In quick time I set up a try and scored one, and then slotted a field goal on the stroke of half-time to pull us back to 18–13.

In the sheds, Malcolm patted me on the back and apologised for playing me off the bench. I reminded him, 'Never underestimate a champion.' I forgave Mal. Being English, he wasn't used to dealing with genius.

Although we were behind, we were super-confident of beating the Eels. Early in the second half, Barge-Arse Johns kicked a penalty goal and with the score 18–15, the Parra boys were shitting in their pants. The next 20 minutes was hard-fought and tough.

Both sides knew whoever scored next would probably kick away and snatch the semi. This is a time when champions – or magicians, or whatever you like to call me – step up and stamp their class on a game.

I got the ball on halfway, dummied, and put on the famous Reagan body swerve, which bamboozled my mortal opponents. Now there was only the fullback, Luke Burt, to beat. I could have stepped him, or trampled over the top of him, but typically I chose to be unselfish and gave Mr Dally-M-winner Andrew Johns a clear run for the line for the winning try.

But then came high drama. As Johns planted the ball down, Parramatta's Jason Smith raced in and collected our illustrious No. 7 in the ribs with his knees. Johns screamed with agony. I screamed with laughter.

The halfback was carted off the field, and without his grandstanding and ball-hogging we were able to step up a gear, and never looked back. We went on to win the game comfortably.

Our next opponent was North Sydney, with the winner to face the shit-hot Manly Sea Eagles in the grand final. All the media talked about in the lead-up to the match was whether Joey Bloody Johns's little rib injury would prevent him from playing. He made a big deal about bravely getting off his deathbed to play because the boys couldn't win without him.

The match was played in bloody awful conditions. Sydney Football Stadium was a mudheap after a week of heavy rain and a Let's Get Nude For Lower Petrol Prices rally, which was held there the day before. Our first half was excellent. We were in complete charge. Or, at least, I was. Because it was wet and slippery, I reverted to my masterful kick-and-chase game, which had us ahead 14–6 at half-time.

Shortly after the break, Andrew Johns caused another sensation. He had a bad reaction to his painkilling injection and had to be replaced. Suddenly the Bears were inspired, and came at us hard and drew level. With seven minutes left to play, it was 14–14. For the next five minutes, both sides attacked and defended as if their lives depended on it. Modesty prevents me from telling in full detail how, with two minutes to go, a certain Sir Reg Reagan sipped from the goblet of courage and won the day for his team.

Suffice to say, we were camped on our line. It was the fourth tackle. I knew this would be our last set and that something super-special was needed right then and there. I took the ball at first receiver, dummied to Bill Peden, and in one motion stepped and kick-chipped over the defence. Bears defenders tried to shoulder me from the ball, but I shrugged them aside and picked up the ball one-handed from the sticky mudheap. With little room to move, I then accelerated and escaped the clutches of Norths' Jason Taylor. Next, I ran towards halfway with only their fullback, Matt Seers, to beat. Once more I put my pedal to the metal and . . . tragedy struck! I felt my hamstring tear. I was in terrible pain and stopped dead on halfway. Would this disaster rob us of our grand-final berth? No f**kin' chance.

Champions always find a way to turn a negative into

a positive. I couldn't run. There was no one to pass to because I'd left my teammates in my dust back on our goal-line. Seers, knowing I was wounded, sprinted to hammer me. Then came my masterstroke. I performed a subtle head-fake to the right and transferred all my weight to the left. This gained me a valuable few seconds. With that, I dropped the ball onto my right foot and attempted a miracle field goal from 50 metres out. The moment the ball left my boot I knew it would go over. It sailed gloriously between the uprights. The Knights were going to make their first grand final appearance. The *Daily Telegraph* headlined with 'Reagan Josh: Oh, What A Dish!'. The *Sydney Morning Herald* raved 'Manly Reg Ready For Sea Eagles!'. *The Australian Women's Weekly* proclaimed 'Reg For Governor-General!'.

The city of Newcastle exploded with grand-final fever. Each day the *Herald* plastered pictures of me on its front and back pages. Each night I plastered myself at the pub as I focused on the great challenge that lay ahead. Manly had beaten us in our past 11 encounters but I had taken no part in any of these. So, as far as I was concerned, that statistic wasn't worth a piece of shit.

Little Joey Johns decided he needed to spend the week in hospital trying to convince all and sundry that he had a punctured lung. And at the end of the week he was declared a hero when he emerged from his tomb to announce that he'd play with the help of a painkiller.

Fair dinkum, all the fuss about Johns made me sick. People didn't have a clue what *I* was going through just to get onto the paddock. Unlike Joey, I didn't seek sympathy and attention, so I said nothing about how I was suffering the worst case of haemorrhoids ever recorded. My arsehole looked like a friggin' vineyard. Just to warm up, I needed 16 needles in my rectum to dull the sweet ache.

Grand-final day arrived and we were really pumped. Even so, in the sheds before the game we tried to treat the Big One like any other. Some of the boys listened to rap music, some fiddled nervously with a football, some drank kava. Me, I always find it relaxing before a crucial game to read my headlines – usually at the top of my voice – so it was pretty much business as usual.

The game started with a bang. There were plenty of huge hits, a few cheap shots and a punch-up or two. It was great stuff and just like being back in the '70s. I revelled in the madness and taught some of my inexperienced opponents a thing or two. Just like when I was in the trenches with Tommy and Les, I kicked, elbowed, gouged and grabbed testicles. I hadn't grabbed so many genitals since my navy days.

Incredibly, we left the field at half-time down 14–6. In the dressing room, panic spread through the team. All the blaming and finger-pointing that was going on – it was like the Spanish Inquisition. Something had to be done, so I stood up and told the boys: 'Shut up! Save your energy. This mindless squabbling is doing us no good at all. Now, it's important that we block out those areas where we've been below our best.' For instance, Marc Glanville had forgotten how to tackle, and Mark Hughes had forgotten how to play.

We started the second half in much better fashion. It brought a tear to my eye to see the game being played in such a tough but sporting manner. Except, of course, when Mad Dog McDougall trampled on Geoff Toovey's face, and John Hopoate used his index finger to check Adam Muir's temperature, veterinary-style.

With 15 minutes left on the clock, the match intensified. At one stage there were three or four separate fights going on. Lyons vs Crowe, Harragon vs Carroll, Reagan vs the Manly cheer squad. Robbie O'Davis took advantage of all the mayhem to tip-toe through the defence to score his second try of the match and level the scores.

Only five minutes to go, and I tried to pot a few field goals, but my haemorrhoids were effecting my follow-through and, unlike the week before, the ball just wasn't leaving my foot sweetly. Having my boots on the wrong feet may also have been a factor. With 60 seconds left, there was a stoppage in play. It was now or never. I fronted Andrew Johns. 'Listen, you little bastard,' I growled, 'all these Manly blokes are sweating on me to do something brilliant. I'll give you a tip. Late in the tackle count throw a dummy to me, skip down the short side and let's just say you might get a little surprise.' Johns looked confused, but promised he'd try to follow my orders.

With 40 seconds left we were in possession in Manly's half. As the ball travelled towards the right touchline, Johns yelled to me: 'Reg, I can't do it! You do the big play!' He was on the verge of tears. 'I'm tired, Reg. I'm sore. My ribs are hurting!'

I ran over and grabbed him by the jumper. 'Listen, son,' I roared, 'life is about taking your opportunities. Sure, I could pull this off and be Newcastle's hero for yet another week, but to tell you the truth, I'm sick of all the hero worship. I'm giving you the opportunity of a lifetime. Now, take it!'

The hapless No. 7 was obviously shaken by my tongue-lashing. He waddled across to the ball as our winger, Darren Albert, was tackled 10 metres out from Manly's line. I took my position in centrefield and gave a dummy call for the ball. The Manly boys, knowing I was Newcastle's danger man, converged on me. Then Andrew Johns, that selfish little bugger, made me proud. He threw me a beaut dummy and, as I got smashed by about six Sea Eagles, he ventured down the short side, found Albert inside him, and the winger touched down for the winning try with two seconds left on the clock.

Sydney Football Stadium erupted. Hysterical fans invaded the field. Strangers hugged. Touch judges kissed. Andrew Johns sobbed uncontrollably as he threw his arms around me and thanked me for my genius. Suddenly, the media stormed onto the ground and a camera was shoved in Johns's face. The Channel Nine reporter asked Joey what was going on in his head when he executed that last play. Surely Johns would give me the credit I deserved. I puffed out my chest in anticipation and pondered how I'd deal with all the glory, not to mention the Order of Australia Medal that would surely be coming my way.

But no. 'Mate, I can't explain how I did what I did,' Johns crowed. 'I just sensed something was on and went for it.'

I was stunned. Somehow I was able to keep smiling for the cameras, gave Johns a hug and whispered in his ear, 'Get ready for a hiding, you ungrateful prick!'

In the end I let him off the hook. By the time we reached the sheds I couldn't have given a shit. All I cared about was that I had a grand-final ring on my finger and I was going to get drunk for six months. I had loved being a Newcastle Knight, but it was time to move on. So, off I strode into the sunset, leaving behind many good memories and 184 paternity suits.

16
HELLO, WORLD – IT'S REG REAGAN!

IT'S ONLY NATURAL. When your name is constantly appearing in huge newspaper headlines and your face is on the telly more than Jamie Dury's and Kerri-Anne Kennerly's combined, you get to learn a lot about show biz and how it works. For some time I'd harboured a secret desire to have a crack at being a media star, and I figured that with all my knowledge and talent the moment was right to make my move into the spotlight.

My appetite for writing was whetted when the American actor and cultural icon Mr T asked me to ghostwrite his autobiography. I met T when I was working as an extra on the set of *The A-Team*. About that time, I was going through a very political period of my life and I'd strut around the *A-Team* location in a Malcolm X T-shirt. In my spare time I'd lie for hours in Hollywood solariums getting a deep tan, so I'd be

'John who?' After locking Lawsy out of the studio, 2UE finally got the ratings they only dreamed of.

mistaken for an Afro-American. Mr T really respected this, of course, and I'd hang with him and the rest of the Boyz around the clubs of LA. Eventually I had to return to Australia for pre-season training, but Mr T and I knew we'd be mates for life.

Sure enough, one day he telephoned out of the blue and asked me to pen his memoirs. I was honoured, but puzzled. I mean, apart from doing *The A-Team*, getting the shit pounded out of him in *Rocky III*, and starring in a couple of F-grade movies, what had he ever f**kin' done?

Still, I copped the money and launched into my task with great enthusiasm, and I was pretty proud of the book on its completion. Needless to say, it sold like hotcakes in the US, and European sales were steady.

Then Mr T and his publisher called and asked me to take control of the book's promotion, because it was soon to be released in Australia and Asia. I agreed, and it was enjoyable but incredibly tiring work. I was interviewed for TV, radio and the newspapers and magazines. I did bookshop signing sessions and organised quirky little stunts such as the *Mr T Movie Marathon*, which the Nine Network agreed to show between 2–5 am. Soon there was only one engagement remaining, a guest appearance on the great John Laws's nationally broadcast morning radio talkback program.

Being the kind of bloke I am, I envy nobody, but I'd always been mighty impressed by Laws and the way he worked. A small part of me wanted to be like him. Some nights I'd sit at the pub, close my eyes and pretend that my Chiko Roll was the 2UE microphone . . . 'Hello, World . . . This is John Laws. C'mon, give me a call and tell me what's going on in this big, brown beautiful land.'

I knew Lawsy well. Quite a few years back he'd dated my

sister, Regan, and for a while there I thought he was going to be part of the clan. We all lived in a little two-bedroom fibro, so it's fair to say that during John and Regan's fling, I got to experience some of his more intimate interviews.

Each night I was entertained by Lawsy's commentary as he let Regan handle his Golden Microphone. 'And how does it feel, my fine young Australian goddess,' he'd rumble in that lowdown register.

He and I were pretty good mates. I was only a young bloke, but if you're old enough to listen to a fella bonk, you're old enough to enjoy a beer with him. John took me to the movies, taught me to ride a horse and write poetry, and even showed me how to play the guitar.

But I must admit, I was a little nervous about meeting Lawsy again to promote Mr T's book, because things didn't end so good between John and Regan. After he broke it off, the old man and I went around and paid Lawsy a visit. I tried to explain what a wonderful little woman he was throwing away, while Dad broke his ribs and drilled a hole in each of the great man's kneecaps.

Yet, when I walked into 2UE that day, the radio legend greeted me like a long-lost brother. We sat and chatted about old times for what felt like two minutes. John even asked after Regan. I had to tell him the truth, that being dumped by him had turned her into a chronically depressed lesbian who sat in her room all day with the blinds down listening to k.d. lang CDs.

Lawsy warmly invited me into his studio for our interview and, frankly, I was blown away by the surge of adrenalin that coursed through me when I took my seat behind the microphone. The interview went great. I was wowing John with hilarious anecdotes from the book, and he was enjoying having me as his guest so much that he asked me to stay on and continue entertaining his listeners after the commercial break. As the ads were playing, he said to me: 'Reg, this is great stuff. I'm just popping out into the corridor to grab a glass of water. Want one?'

'Sure, John,' I replied. 'Very kind of you.'

As he removed his headphones and left the studio, an idea hit me like a Clubber Lang left to the jaw. Here was my big chance! Right then, I had millions of Australians glued to their radios. The power had totally intoxicated me and I seized the moment! Leaping from the guest stool with blinding speed, I bolted the studio door. When Lawsy saw that I'd locked him out, he tried to break in. He couldn't. *I* was in control. I was the new Golden Tonsils.

'Ah hah!' I yelled with a triumphant grin. 'Payback time! You screwed my sister, now you can watch me root your radio program!'

Then I sat myself down in his beautiful Italian leather chair. In front of me hung a glorious gleaming boom microphone, the kind of implement any man would kill to have hanging between his knees. I looked at the switchboard and it was twinkling with little red lights, each one a caller desperate to tell their story to yours truly and benefit from my wisdom.

I leaned slowly forward, took a deep breath, and allowed my moustache to gently caress the great phallic symbol on my panel. 'Hello, World,' I intoned, 'this is Reg Reagan. Lawsy has fallen ill and asked me to step into the breach today. So, c'mon, give me a call, 'cause it's a beautiful bloody day outside. Let's go! What do you want to talk about?

Education? Interest rates? World peace? Don't waste a moment. Give me a call. Let me apply some Dencorub to your troubled souls.'

The first hour of the Reg Reagan show went fantastically well. The ratings were phenomenal, the highest in Australian radio history. It felt so empowering, helping people out, brightening up their meaningless lives.

But I soon discovered that being a talkback radio star is not as easy as it looks. I found it was difficult to maintain concentration and listen intently with caller after caller bombarding the line. By the two-hour mark my attention was wandering and I was on automatic pilot. This led to a minor incident.

A lovely old lady rang and asked what she should do about her dog. She told me he was getting on in years, was blind and had arthritis, and just lay around the house all day. To me it was a no-brainer, and I told her in no uncertain terms that if she loved the old bugger the kindest thing she could do was put him down straight away. She followed my advice to the letter. It was great radio to hear the shotgun go off in the background.

Well, you wouldn't believe it but 15 minutes later there was a tremendous banging on the studio door. At first I thought it was Lawsy, but it was the police. They'd come to arrest me. Turns out the old dear wasn't talking about her sick dog, but about her husband, Doug. I'd misheard her – a mistake anyone could make. I explained everything to the cops, and they had a good old chuckle and took off.

Lawsy was humiliated, and furious about my, as he called it, 'treacherous hijacking' of his show, but 2UE management were doing cartwheels of joy as the ratings soared throughout the morning. Australia loved me. I juggled calls, sang some grand old bush ballads, like the Cessnock Goannas club song, and told insightful anecdotes about my numerous sporting triumphs. As word spread through Sydney and all over the land via 2UE's sister stations, the ratings rocketed even higher. 'Reg, can you keep it up till four?' pleaded the station honchos.

'I've got nothing better to do today,' I replied. 'You know where to send the cheque.'

Australia's high-flyers were of course tripping over themselves to cash in on my celebrity and success, and made a beeline to the studio to be guests on my show. The pathetic bastards were lined up out of the 2UE building and on down the Pacific Highway. You name 'em, they were there. Shane Warne, Alan Bond, Alexander Downer . . .

South African Archbishop Desmond Tutu dribbled on for a while. This bloke could really talk bullshit. At one point Tutu had the nerve to remark that to be a really good person you must love everyone. 'What? Even fat, ugly sheilas?' was my well-considered response, and I told Tutu to piss off out of my studio.

The next celebrity to grace the show was Prime Minister John Howard. I took him to task big-time. I demanded to know why he hadn't legalised marijuana and prostitution. After about 10 more minutes of such erudite banter, Little Johnny suddenly hurled his headphones down and stormed out of the studio. If you ask me, he had a massive overreaction to my innocent suggestion that his idea of an alliance with the United States was being dragged into the Oval Office and getting a look-no-hands cavity search by the George Bushes Snr and Jnr.

All in all, I enjoyed my day as a top-rating broadcaster, but it wore me out. I made it through to 4 pm, and just after I signed off, the boss of 2UE cornered me and offered a squillion-buck contract to do my show every weekday for the next five years. For anyone else, this would have been a once-in-a-lifetime opportunity, but, as I explained to him, I had too many other mountains to climb, and besides, I believed my show biz future lay in television – my handsome face was wasted on radio.

As for Lawsy, there were no real hard feelings. He broke my sister's heart. I destroyed his career. We were square, and to this day John and I laugh about it all over a beer.

As I left the radio station, the street outside was filled with people of all ages screaming my name. They wanted to thank me for bringing the biff back to broadcasting. The praise went on and on. Later in the year I was named Electronic Media Presenter Of The Year. Naturally, I dedicated my award to Lawsy.

Not a week goes by when a radio station doesn't try to woo me back behind the microphone. I politely tell 'em to shove it up their arses. It's best if radio remains just another special memory for me, and for the many millions who were lucky enough to tune in on that landmark day.

17

A NIGHT AT THE OPRAH

BELIEVE ME, I've seen all the diet fads. The Low Carbohydrate Diet. The High Protein and the Zig-Zag Diet, the Cabbage Diet, the Detox Diet, the Cold Gold KB Diet. You name it – Reg has seen it and Reg has done it.

Not a day passes without everyday people, mostly good-looking sheilas, coming up and saying, 'Reg,' – or 'Mr Reagan', as I prefer the public to address me – 'how do you stay in such buffed shape?'

I always tell 'em that, for me, it's all about genetics. I guess I'm lucky because I come from a perfect gene pool, which guarantees good looks and a perfect physique. But others – let's say 99.9 per cent of the Australian population – are not so fortunate. Their lives must fall to pieces every time they look in the mirror and see a rough head sitting on Jabba the Hutt's body. For them, I'm afraid, life is corn

COMPLETELY UPDATED!
The Must-Have NEW Edition

RUN, YOU' FAT PRICK!

completely unaccredited advice

- Tips on how not to be completely worthless
- Unfat your pitiful life
- Wearing black doesn't always make you look slimmer

Reg Reagan

REVISED and IMPROVED

Some people loved my book so much they chose to be buried with it.

chips and masturbation. They must get sick and tired of leaving nightclubs with nothing but the taste of rum and Diet Coke on their breath and a greasy doner kebab in their hand.

People, I feel your pain. I know you're sick of the indignity of being pig-fat, and I know you need a good-natured stranger like me to wipe your arse. So, here I am to help. And that's just what I told Oprah Winfrey when she invited me on her top-rating US television talk show, to help Americans get the body they dream about. No, not mine. I mean the one they have hidden somewhere under 150 kilos of ugly fast-food and couch-potato blubber.

I've kept a transcript of my appearance (which was lucky in the light of her many subsequent attempts to sue my sorry butt for having her show booted off the airwaves), and am happy to reproduce it here . . .

> OPRAH: Reg, welcome to the show.
> REG: Darl, any time.
> OPRAH: Reg, I guess I'm like most people. I have trouble controlling my weight, but I . . .
> REG: You sure do. About six months ago I mentioned to the missus you looked almost healthy, but I noticed when we first met back there in the green room this evening, that your arse has almost tripled in size!
> OPRAH: Thanks for noticing . . .
> REG: Hard not to, darl!
> OPRAH: Moving on . . . Reg, on my show we've had all types of diets put forward. Even those that work never seem to keep the weight off for long. Why is that?
> REG: Now, Ops, I'm a straight-shooter. The thing is,

Miss Winfrey, that you and all your fat, lazy countrymen and women are a bunch of soft cocks!!

OPRAH: Excuse me?

REG: You heard me: SOFT COCKS!

OPRAH: Uh, I don't understand . . .

REG: No, you wouldn't, and nor would your halfwit viewers. You people sit around all day on your massive rear ends working out the best way to feed your face without getting off the couch. Trying to find a miracle diet that can help you look like f**king Elle Mac-f**king-pherson without breaking into a sweat! Am I right? Too right, I'm right!

OPRAH: Mr Reagan, I must warn you. Your foul language will not be tolerated on . . .

REG: Aw, stick it! You know I'm right! You wanna know how to lose weight? You turn off the TV, walk out your front door, and you keep f**king walking!

OPRAH: Mr Reagan, again, your language!

REG: I'll say it one more time: YOU KEEP F**KING WALKING! Until you find a steep hill and then you keep running up and down the friggin' thing!

OPRAH: When do you stop?

REG: You stop when you wake up in the back of an ambulance with a drip hangin' out of your arm.

OPRAH: Mr Reagan, are you finished?

REG: No, I haven't plugged my diet book yet. Viewers, if you want to learn about the one and only way to lose that flab, buy my book, *Run, You Fat Prick!* It's available in all good bookstores. And, Oprah, I'll give you this signed copy absolutely free.

A Night at the Oprah

Among mates, I can reveal that in spite of me tirelessly promoting it, my book was never a bestseller. Yet, those people who did apply my dieting methods achieved amazing results. Yes, many of them died, but I understand their weight loss was appreciated by the pallbearers.

18

THE EDUCATION OF BOBBY DE NIRO

THAT VISIT TO THE US, hawking my diet book, brawling in nightclubs and screwing anything that moved, was an unforgettable experience for a little bloke from the Australian sticks, but I've never been able to work out why I won so few friends. Maybe the Yanks are different to us. You want a personal point of view? Honestly, I didn't like the Americans. The birds had big arses, the blokes had big mouths, and the beer was like something you'd find at the bottom of a Cessnock outfall pipe – believe me, I've drunk from one.

But the way I see it, if you can make one great friendship on a trip, then it's all worthwhile. My appearance on *The Oprah Winfrey Show* was by no means the only time I've mixed with show-biz royalty.

The greenroom at Johnny Carson's *Tonight Show* studio

'You lookin' at me?' Me and Bobby on our way to the Cessnock RSL.

was a small lounge where we superstars, and other guests, were sent to relax and exchange insider celebrity gossip before we went on air. The day I was there it was filled with the rich and famous.

In one corner of the room sat Valerie Perrine, who – I have to say it – couldn't take her eyes off my genital region. Not even the footy shorts I was wearing could camouflage my mighty schlong. It was getting a bit embarrassing for the other guests as Valerie drooled, her eyes bulging out of her head. I thought I'd put her out of her misery as well as give her a bit of a thrill, and sneakily slipped one of my nuts out of the side of my daks. Well, who knows if she'd just remembered a pressing engagement elsewhere, or had a panic attack at having to appear on national TV, but Valerie screamed and ran from the room.

Muscleman action hero Arnold Schwarzenegger was sitting there too, with Maria Shriver. He was big-noting about how he was Hollywood's ideal boyfriend because he never went anywhere without his girlfriend under his arm. He flexed his huge steroid-boosted bicep to emphasise the boast. I chimed in, 'Yeah, well, Arnie, give it a few years, and I reckon a dialysis machine will be making it a threesome!'

Schwarzenegger stood up and stared at me, and put on a bit of bluff. Was I intimidated? Nope. 'F**k off, Arnie!' I snapped at the future Governor of California, 'a bloke with cashew-sized testicles doesn't scare me.'

I chatted with Elton John for a while. Unlike Arnie, Elt wasn't a bad bloke. I told him I loved his music and had a few of his LPs at home. He was deeply touched after I announced that one of my favourite Elton John songs, 'Werewolves Of London', was nearly Ruth's and my wedding waltz.

I was having a ball, cracking jokes, telling stories. Modesty aside, I was on fire. Unbelievably, not everyone appreciated me. There were a few other musos and B-grade celebrities there, but they were all up themselves, and rolled their eyes and growled in disgust as I held the floor. Donald 'High-and-Mighty' Sutherland excused himself to go to the loo. Don left his coffee on a table by his chair, so I seized my chance. 'Hey, everyone, watch this,' I yelled. At that, I dropped my strides and pulled out my prick, which at the time was covered in some weird little green spots that eventually went away, and pissed in the star's coffee.

When Sutherland returned, those other gutless so-called celebrities just sat there, too horrified to warn him. He was about to drink from his piss-filled cup when the only decent person in the room stepped in. 'I wouldn't drink that, Mr Sutherland,' I remarked.

'Why not, my dear fellow?'

'Well, while you were gone, Arnie had a 'roid rage and urinated in your coffee.'

The acclaimed thespian sniffed his polluted beverage and roared, 'You filthy Austrian!' and hurled the steaming coffee in Arnie's face.

'Eeek! Maria, Maria, help me!' squealed Conan the Barbarian.

I was cacking myself, rolling around on the floor of Johnny's greenroom as Arnie went to water. I couldn't help chipping in, 'Vart's da madder, Arnuld, got a toomar!'

All the Hollywood crowd pissed off. Arnie rushed straight to his therapist. Then I noticed there was one person left in the room. A small bloke with a goatee and bushy eyebrows, he sat there absolutely hosing himself with laughter. I shook his hand and said: 'Reg Reagan from Cessnock. Pleased to meet you, Mr Scorsese. I'm glad someone's got a sense of humour.'

'Man, it's an honour to shake your hand, you are one f**kin' hardcore, twisted individual,' he said in his famous high-pitched, rapid-fire New York twang. 'Nice to meet ya. Call me Marty.'

I was immediately impressed by the great director's firm handshake and psycho eyes under those brows that made John Howard's look like anorexic caterpillars. We chatted for a while and he asked if I was free to catch up for a drink at his local bar later that night. Was I!

Marty's boozer was right out of his classic movies *Mean Streets* and *Taxi Driver*. There was a lap dancer who, for one shocking moment, I mistook for Mum; she had similar tattoos on her chest. A drunken wog crooner in the worst wig I've ever seen was murdering 'You Light Up My Life' and there was skuzzy evil-smelling grime on the floor and walls. The stench of stale beer and sweat was in the air. The women customers were fat, sleazy and ugly and the barkeep didn't talk, he growled. I was in heaven.

Marty ordered a couple of bottles of the usual Yankee horse piss and we sat in the corner and chewed the fat. Soon I realised he had a reason for luring me to this bar. And no, it wasn't to have sex with me. Years later, he explained all in his bestselling autobiography, *Goodfellas & Muthaf**kers*:

> *When I first set eyes on the great Australian Reg Reagan, I liked him. I liked his look — there was something manly and somehow attractively dangerous about the way he humiliated Arnold Schwarzenegger. I was about to start shooting* Raging Bull, *a movie about the life of former*

world champion middleweight boxer Jake LaMotta. Robert De Niro, who'd starred in several of my films, was a natural for the lead role, but about the time I bumped into Reg, we'd come to a dead halt. Problem was, Bobby was a slim man and while this was OK for the boxing scenes, for half of the shoot he had to stack on 55 pounds to portray LaMotta as an old guy who'd retired from the ring and become a slob. Well, in those months before I yelled 'Action!' on Raging Bull *we tried every weight-gain diet, but nothing worked. We were staring disaster in the face. We had just eight weeks to turn Bobby into a lard-guts or the moneymen would pull the funding for the entire film.*

I was clueless. Then I took one look at the way Reg's monstrous gut hung over his football shorts and thought, 'Whatever this guy's done to himself, that's what De Niro has to do.' So, although I was a little scared of Reg's foul temper and fouler language, I made my pitch to this strange Aussie throwback to the Neanderthal age. 'Unless Bobby bloats up, we're sunk,' I told Reg. I pleaded with him to take the intense master actor under his wing for a few months and make De Niro live, eat, drink and play the Reagan way. Money was no object, I'd pay all expenses. I was elated when Reg said he'd be glad to help out.

Well, I was looking forward to meeting Robert De Niro. I'd liked him in *Taxi Driver*. His character, Travis Bickle, who kept an arsenal in his bedroom and went to porn flicks, reminded me of my dad, Ray.

So there I was in my hotel room on the morning of my return to Australia, contemplating one more quick beer before heading for LAX, when there was a knock on the door. I opened it, and I was face to face with Scorsese and the great Robert De Niro.

Bob was nice enough, but I could tell that shacking up with me in Cessnock for the next two months was not sky-high on his list of things he wanted to do. I did my best to reassure him: 'Hey, relax, Bobby. I give you my word I won't make you do anything I can't and I reckon that if you give it a week or two, you'll love downtown Cessnock as much as I do.'

De Niro attempted to argue the point, but Scorsese cut him short. 'Bobby, get this into your head, muthaf**ker, Reg is the boss. What he says goes. If you have a problem with that, I'll sack you from the movie and replace you with Gary Coleman.'

De Niro had a healthy ego, and it bloody well grew even more inflated on the flight over as he was bothered by a succession of grovelling autograph hunters. He must have signed 200 arses and 400 tits. But what really pissed me off was that yours truly, sports legend and bestselling author, was completely ignored by these bottom-feeding fans.

When De Niro and I landed in Sydney, I hired a car and we set off on the two-hour drive to Cessnock. On the way, we chatted candidly and got along well. We both enjoyed a drink and a feed, and got off on extreme violence. I was very impressed by Bobby's stories of Hollywood fame and fortune, but pretended that I couldn't give a shit. When he droned on about winning an Oscar for *The Godfather Part II* at the 1974 Academy Awards, I interrupted him with a laugh. 'Mate,' I said, 'save your breath. Oscar Schmoscar. You haven't been to an awards night until you've been to the Country Rugby League Player of the Year presentation. Play your cards right and you may get a start.' I could tell he was deeply impressed, because he was speechless.

I took advantage of the silence to lay down the law. 'Now, Mr Bigtime Hollywood Actor,' I barked, 'this ain't a holiday. You're in for a rugged time. As far as I'm concerned we're going into camp for two months and you're going to suffer and sweat, and there'll be times when you'll beg me to lay off. I can promise you pain and misery. And something else, too! If you do what I say, do what I do, and eat and drink what I eat, at the end of eight weeks you'll look like John Candy, and the Best Actor Oscar for *Raging Bull* will be as good as yours.'

Understanding how serious I was about the job Martin Scorsese had entrusted me to do, Ruth had moved out to stay at her mother's. It was just De Niro and me at my little two-bedroom fibro bungalow. Things began badly. I could see he was a tad put out that my home had none of the luxury he was accustomed to. Then he laid eyes on Ruth's and my cosy bed. 'Uh-uh, sleeping in beds is for poofters!' I snapped at him, and marched straight out into the backyard and pitched a two-man tent. This would be our sleeping quarters at Stalag Reagan.

Next day I put my weight-gain program into operation. I began by asking Bobby about his usual diet. 'What do you have for breakfast?' I asked.

He thought about it, and replied in that barely understandable mumble of his, 'Ah, some cereal, err, a bit of fruit and a coffee.'

'You soft prick,' I scoffed. 'From now on, brekky will be two T-bone steaks, two fried eggs and a bowl of pork crackling washed down with a schooner of green ginger wine. Now, lunch?'

'Err, maybe a ham sandwich or, like, an omelette.'

THIS IS MY LIFE!

I glared at De Niro with disdain. 'Well, Mr 40-Hour Famine, for lunch at Chez Reagan you'll be having 12 party pies, two Chiko Rolls, four cream horns (with mock cream and a maraschino cherry), and a bottle of Malibu!'

'Ah,' said Bobby, who was turning green at the thought of my carefully planned menus, 'and what about dinner?'

'Easy,' I said, 'I'm gonna take you to the RSL for the Chinese smorgasbord. I'm gonna chain you to your Laminex table and force-feed you sweet and sour sauce until it trickles out of your arse! Any questions?'

'What about my, um, cholesterol?'

It was time for some tough love. 'I've had enough of your lack of dedication!' I shouted at Bobby. 'Now, listen here, you dirty little Itie. You may think life is about eating your mama's pasta, tongue-kissing your aunties and buggering domestic animals! But now you're in the real world, *my* world! Look around you, Bob, there are no servants, no French champagne, not even a colour TV. There's just you, me, a two-man tent and a packet of Trojan condoms in case you get lonely.'

This little pep talk snapped De Niro back to reality, and the actor took to his new surroundings and exercise regime like a wog to vino. We'd wake each morning and he'd rip into his breakfast. Then we'd struggle over to our matching banana chairs, and lie around watching the soaps. All that time, I'd make him graze on chocolate, potato chips and ice cream.

In the arvos, after lunch, we'd drive 20 metres down the road to the pinball parlour, and plonk our arses on stools while we pinged and flipped away at the little steel balls and drank milkshake after milkshake. When it got dark we'd drive next door to the RSL for our Chinese feast, then catch a cab around the block to Peden's Hotel at about 7 pm to drink ourselves into oblivion until we got chucked out at closing time. Then it was back to the tent to regather our energy for the following day.

After two weeks of this routine, Bobby had gained 6 kilograms. De Niro was looking more and more like Jake LaMotta, but the problem was that when the time came for him to lose the weight and play Jake as a young bloke he'd have to know how to fight, and he didn't have a clue how to hold his hands up. Bobby was f**kin' embarrassing. He might have been part Italian, but he was no Rocky Balboa. In fact, he was more like Rocky Dennis. His limp-wristed punches packed the power of a Christmas beetle.

Oh well, I figured, nothing else to do but add boxing lessons to our eating-and-slobbing-around regime. Each day at Cessnock Police Boys Club, we'd go a few rounds in the ring, and I found it tremendously empowering punching the crap out of an Academy Award winner.

After a few more weeks, Bobby had gained another 5 kilograms and was getting better in the ring as well. But, all in all, he was still a shithouse fighter. I knew that for him to reach the level where he could convince moviegoers he was a champion boxer, I'd have to resort to extreme methods.

Now, Peden's Hotel had its share of roughnecks and hard arses in those days but because De Niro was there with yours truly, they wisely left him alone, even though I knew deep down that every one of them would have given his wife's left testicle to have a go at the Hollywood hotshot. So I figured I'd give them their chance. After all, I knew nothing would improve Bob's technique like a few old-fashioned all-in pub brawls.

THIS IS MY LIFE!

In the award-winning documentary of his life, *The Education Of An Actor*, De Niro talked about the quality time he and I shared in Cessnock. 'Everything was travelling wonderfully and I was really enjoying my time with Reg,' he told the interviewer. 'I particularly enjoyed our nights at Peden's Hotel, where I started to feel like I was not a million-dollar celebrity but just one of the boys. Then Reg started playing games. One night he told one of the real heavies in the pub, a bloke just out of jail who weighed nearly 450 pounds, that I'd been big-noting about how I'd screwed his wife while he was in the can. I was relieved when the big bastard told Reg that he had to be lying, because his wife was dead. "Oh," said Reg, "then that explains why Bob carries a shovel each night when he leaves the pub!" The heavy beat me senseless and my life was flashing before my eyes. Then Reg stepped in and knocked the bloke cold.

'Every night he'd land me in a fight, and I always copped a hiding that left me bleeding profusely and on the verge of death. Yet, after a week or two, I realised there was method in Reg's madness. Pretty soon I was giving as good as I got, and even notched up a victory or two. I still spent the next half day in hospital recovering from concussion but I was light years ahead of where I'd been only weeks before. I tell you, everybody deserves a friend like Reg Reagan.'

With only a week of our regime to go, De Niro had packed on a whopping 24 kilograms. Martin Scorsese phoned him from Hollywood and when Bobby told him it was Mission: Accomplished, Marty said to stuff the final week with me, and get on the first plane back to the States so they could get a head start on the shoot. To my surprise, Bob told Marty to pull his head in. He planned to stay the distance. Turns out the great star had grown to love Stalag Reagan and life in the little Aussie coalmining town.

It shouldn't have surprised me. We had had an idyllic time together. Eating, drinking and fighting every day and night, and then at weekends we'd splash out and get to Cessnock Sportsground to watch my old club, the Goannas, go round. De Niro would stand on the hill with all the locals shouting abuse at the ref and the opposition players. Once or twice his Latin temperament got him into trouble, like the time the mascot from Newcastle Souths gave us a bit of lip, and Bobby got so incensed he jumped over the fence and gave Leon the Lion a hiding. The elderly woman in the lion suit wanted to press charges but with a bit of gentle persuasion from yours truly, all was forgiven.

Cessnock fell in love with the actor. Everywhere he went, people wanted to shake his hand or give him a blow job. The tent sure got a workout that last week. It would be nothing to see 10 birds in there queueing up for a bit of action with Bobby and his spunky mate. The town was in full party mode and the mayor declared the day of Bob's departure a public holiday. In Cessnock, to this day, 23 August is known as De Niro Day.

Our drive back to Sydney airport, where Bob would catch his flight to LA, was a sad one. Bobby cried.

Finally, the moment came when we had to part. Of course, I was able to keep my emotions in check. The same could not be said for De Niro. He hugged me, squeezed me, even tried to stick his tongue down my throat. I sympathised with him, but was forced to call airport security, who dragged him screaming and kicking through customs and hurled him into the first-class compartment of his plane.

On the lonely drive back up the coast, I thought of all the great experiences Bobby and I had shared: the boxing lessons; the piss-ups; the nights scoffing gow gees and dim sims at the chows; the chicks; the days at the footy; and best of all, the spirit his charismatic presence gave my hometown. The next day I got a call from Marty Scorsese thanking me for all my work. Bobby arrived back in Hollywood 38 kilograms heavier than when he left. People mistook him for Marlon Brando.

Raging Bull came out to enormous acclaim a year or so later. Critics raved about De Niro's convincing boxing prowess and dedication to his craft in gaining so much weight for the role. On Oscar night, to the surprise of nobody, he won Best Actor.

I was at home watching the ceremony on our 12-inch black and white Admiral TV. My chest swelled with pride as my mate rose from his seat to a standing ovation from fellow stars and made his way to the microphone to receive his little gold statue. I flipped on my tape recorder to catch his acceptance speech: 'Ah, wow! Ah, wow!' he began. 'There are so many people to thank, all the cast and crew of *Raging Bull*. A huge thank you to Marty for his vision and loyalty. Thank you, Joe Pesci. There is no better co-star. Thanks, Jake LaMotta and the LaMotta family for their insight into this true champion. But, most of all, I'd like to thank a very special friend. He taught me how to be tough, how to be dedicated, and that you have to earn the right to achieve greatness. The bastard nearly destroyed my f**kin' liver, but I love him with all my heart. Reg Reagan, this Oscar is *yours*!'

I was stunned, I don't mind saying. I had tears in my eyes. Just like Abbott and Costello, Torvill and Dean, Lillee and Marsh, my great friendship with Robert De Niro has endured, growing stronger with each passing year. Not many people know this, but Bobby flies to Sydney every November and drives up to Cessnock to celebrate Thanksgiving with the Reagan family. Strangely, we never celebrate the f**king thing! It turns out he's been knocking the missus off. Ah, well . . .

19

TURFED OUT

I LOVE MY SPORT . . . And, as you all know, I also love a beer and the odd Winnie Red. But nothing gets my blood pumping like a day at the races. The bookies in the enclosure shitting themselves, the thoroughbreds accelerating at the top of the home turn, the jockeys in a huddle 10 minutes before the race, arms around each other, eyes moist with emotion, figuring how the hell they'll rig the race this week. And the sheilas in their frocks and follow-me-home-and-f**k-me shoes staggering around the grandstand by race seven after a day on the leg-opener. Ah, the track!

Of course, the highlight of the racing calendar is the Spring Racing Carnival, when the top horses go head-to-head in the big races and there's huge bucks up for grabs. It was on a fantastic Caulfield Cup afternoon a few years back that ol' Reggie Boy decided he was wasting his time and

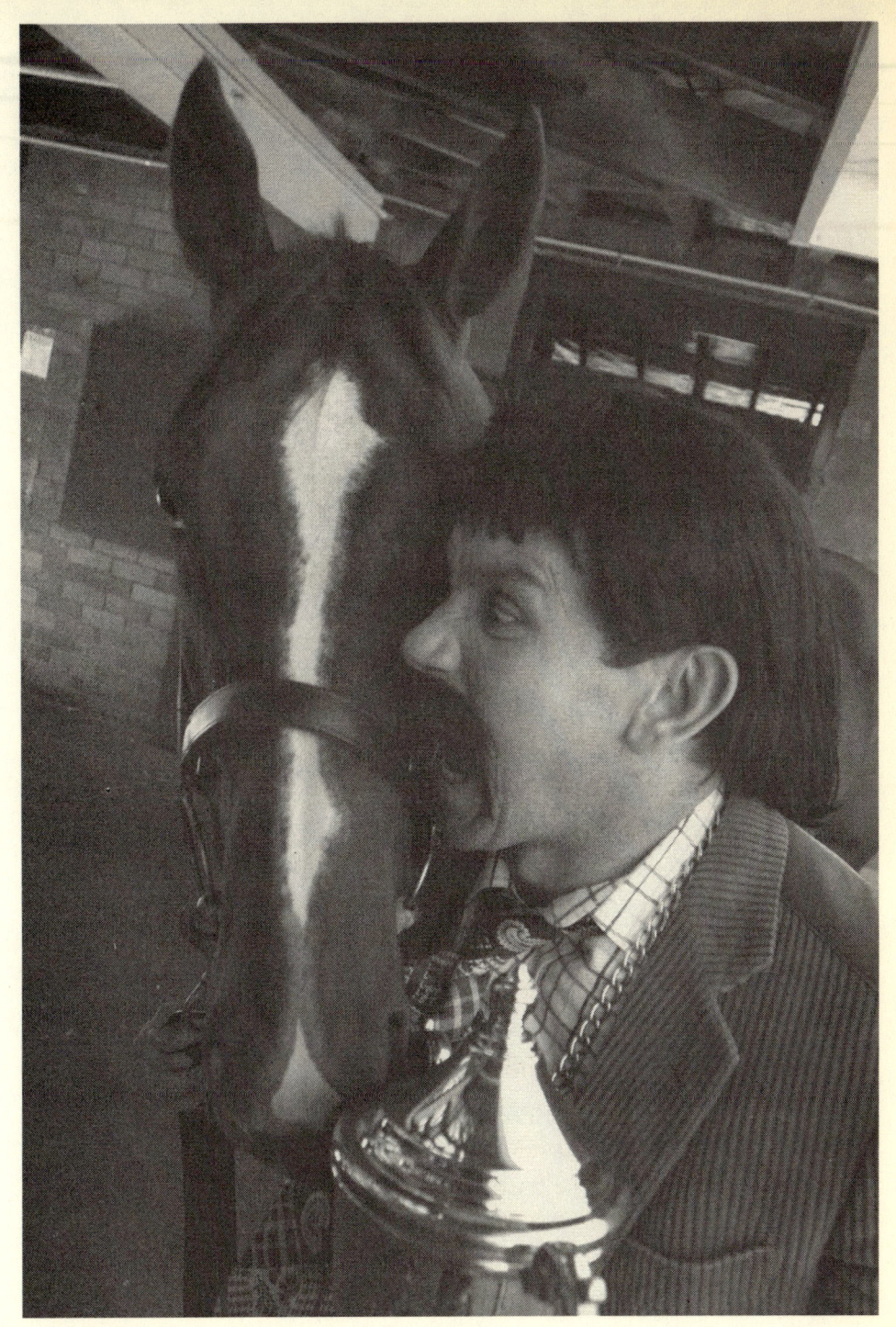

Blood brothers... It's the Melbourne Cup, and here's me telling 'the Prong' how proud I am of him – and that I just remembered the phone number of my contact at Lucky Dog.

THIS IS MY LIFE!

money just being a punter. As successful as I was, the really big dollars and prestige belonged to the blokes who owned the horses. So, that's exactly what I set out to do.

My first priority was finding the right horse to buy, so I hitched up to the Gold Coast when the big sales were on to check out the flesh for myself.

I was cashed up. I'd made a nice sum when I put all the loot I got for winning the '82 Country Rugby League Player of the Year Award in Velcro shares. Amazingly, the stuff went from 10 cents a share to $4.50 overnight. As I hitched through Crescent Head and Murwillumbah, I knew something special was about to happen.

I couldn't believe the money that buyers were paying for thoroughbreds at the sales. I saw sums of $500,000 and $600,000 change hands. Now, I couldn't compete with the chequebooks of these big-spending, big-noting penis biters, but what gave me the edge over them was my uncanny eye for champion horseflesh.

Even so, I almost didn't pull off the buy of the decade. It was late afternoon and the sales were just about over for the day. I skolled my 37th KB and was about to say, 'F**k it!' and head to the pub for a much-needed beer, when suddenly this stocky little chestnut was walked into the ring. Of course, the know-it-all wankers pissed themselves laughing. But old Reg didn't laugh. One look was enough to tell me that this horse was the four-legged payday I'd always dreamed about. The twinkle in his eye and the length of his schlong told me that this little battler and yours truly had plenty in common.

I just had to have him, so decided I'd really go for it and spend my entire $800 on the little beauty. I was nervous, but when I got up close and gave him a little scratch under his chin, he looked me in the eye, nodded, neighed, pounded the ground with his hoof, and his penis dropped three-quarters of the way to the floor. I bought that bugger on the spot.

We caught the train back to Sydney, and on the long journey down the coast, I read the riot act to my new investment on what toughness and tenacity are all about. I pointed out to him that success wasn't about size. No, it was about will to win. If he put in the hard yards, like his master had done all his life, anything was possible. The horse sat and listened intently, a picture of concentration.

By the time our train pulled into Central Station, the bond between us was unbreakable. If his heart was only half the size of his prick, I was on a winner.

We shared a taxi back to the one-bedroom apartment at Lilli Pilli I used as my Sydney headquarters. I'll admit it, I slept restlessly that night. Of course, being a great lover, I was used to sharing my bed with strangers, sometimes two or three. But sleeping beside a horse with a 71-centimetre penis was a new experience.

In the morning we boarded a bus for Newcastle. I had a mate up there, a trainer named Kris Lees. He'd offered me one of his stables for as long as I wanted, and I took him up on it. Every horse needs a base, and Kris's joint had some excellent training facilities.

As we approached his new home, I realised I hadn't done something pretty important. I hadn't given my new horse a name. All the great champions of turf history had unforgettable monikers: Phar Lap, Kingston Town, Fine Cotton. What should I call my own champion? It had to have a ring to it. Had to be a handle that celebrated one of his most outstanding attributes. I pondered for some time. Then it hit me like a Les Boyd elbow! Prong O'Plenty.

The name sounded somehow wise. Almost Chinese. And, of course, it fitted him beautifully. When I daydreamed out loud, 'and the Horse of the Year is . . . Prong O'Plenty,' he bristled and bucked. Oh yeah, something pretty special was brewing.

At Kris's, the trainer led the Prong and me to our new headquarters, a modest little stable. To be honest, Prong looked a tad disappointed but I reassured him, 'Hey, if a tiny stable was good enough for Baby Jesus, Prong, old buddy, it'll be good enough for us.'

Time now for a little Reggie psychology. Around the walls of his new home I hung photographs of other great sporting achievers to inspire him. No matter where he looked, he'd see a legend. There was the great racehorse Archer in the winner's circle, Muhammad Ali snarling over an unconscious Sonny Liston, the Don doffing his cap to adoring crowds after scoring his hundredth hundred, yours truly beating the despairing dive of Terry Regan to score the winning try in the Group 17 preliminary final of 1983. How could he fail?

I visited Prong O' Plenty every day, and each time he looked stronger. I asked Kris Lees if he'd consider taking the Prong on a training run. Lees hemmed and haahed. He said he thought my horse looked keen, but unfortunately he was booked up and couldn't spare the time.

Yes, of course I was hurt. But I took a deep breath, put on a brave face, and told Kris: 'Mate, it's OK. I understand.' Then head low, I trudged outside, thinking to myself: 'Reags, you're well and truly rooted now. Good trainers don't grow on trees and, anyway, Leesy is the only trainer you know.'

So I marched back in to Kris's office, determined to sweet-talk him into changing his mind. 'Listen, you bastard,' I began, calling on the old Reg charm, 'you bloody-well *are* training my horse. We've been through so much together, I need you, mate. Please don't let me down!'

Lees put his hands on his hips, smirked and glanced into the stable where Prong O'Plenty stood. 'F**k off!' Lees barked. 'I've got no time for you or your pit pony.'

And, I'm ashamed to say, f**k off I did, straight to the pub. Somehow the more schooners I sank, the clearer the solution to my problem became, and by the 19th beer I'd made a decision. Training horses is a specialist business, is it not? A science requiring years of experience, not to mention a special kind of horsemanship. It was a no-brainer. I'd prove a point to that toerag Kris Lees, and to the world – I would train Prong O'Plenty myself. Lees and his kind could shove all their fancy-dancy training techniques up their arses.

I took the Prong back to grassroots, to the simple but effective methods that had made me a champion. Together we did road runs, beach sprints, shitloads of push-ups, and wound down with a few cold ones at the local after each session.

Another thing Prong O' Plenty and I loved to do was sleep in. Some so-called trainers get their horses out of the hay at 4.30 am for a workout. Not me. Prong and I kicked off each training day just before lunchtime, around 11.15. We stuck to our routine religiously. The alarm would wake us at 10.30 am. I'd pop my first beer and then prepare the Prong a nice breakfast. Not rabbit food either, but good nutritious chow that built muscle and stamina. I rustled up huge servings of bacon, sausages and eggs, all smothered in barbecue sauce. The chunky little bastard ripped through his brekky like he'd just come off Ramadan.

Then the tough work would begin. Poofter horses you see today do their trackwork on cushy grassed tracks. Prong O' Plenty commenced each session with an hour's canter along the bitumen highway from Cessnock to Singleton. Then I'd make him run on the sandhills at Merewether Beach. For a while he'd finish by galloping up and down the steps outside Newcastle Town Hall (I pinched that from *Rocky*.)

I was hoping that our little runs up the Town Hall steps would build community spirit behind him, just as it had done for the Italian Stallion. This turned ugly one day, though, when during a civic ceremony, Prong collided with the lord mayor and smashed his pelvis.

At 2 pm, I'd send my champion horse back to the stables for a quick Steak Diane (fat left on) and a snooze, before our afternoon workout of aerobics and then a movie to get him focused and in a winning frame of mind. *Rocky*, *Chariots of Fire*, *Field of Dreams*, *Days of Thunder*, even bloody *Ice Castles*. He loved them all, and I loved *him*.

At last our intense training program was over and it was time for Prong's first race. I entered him in an event over 1200 metres at Royal Randwick. I thought the distance and the track would suit him.

Of course, in the lead-up to the race the media wanted a piece of us. In an interview with a journalist from the *Sydney Morning Herald*, I spoke about Prong O'Plenty's champion qualities. I always use interviews to wage psychological warfare on rivals and I came up with a terrific way of creating some mystique around the Prong. I knew he'd been born and bred in Mudgee, but when the journo asked me where Prong hailed from, I replied, knowing that European horses were the flavour of the month: 'Mate, he's a wog. He comes from Europe. Bulgaria.'

'I've never heard of racing in Bulgaria,' said the reporter.

'Well, there is,' I shot back smugly. 'I bought him from the King of Bulgaria.'

'I never knew Bulgaria was a monarchy.'

By now I'd had enough of this jerk and ended the interview immediately. He quickly learned how hard it is to ask questions with your micro tape recorder rammed up your arse. 'Come back when you f**king well know what you're talking about, son,' I barked. 'There's nothing worse than a smartarse journo!'

The bloke from the *Herald* ran the story about Prong being Bulgarian, and suddenly all the other trainers were shitting their pants. If rival horses had worn pants they would have shat theirs too.

The bookies made Prong O' Plenty odds-on favourite. Right before the race I took my jockey, Shane Dye, aside and gave him his riding instructions. My advice was brief, but reflected a lifetime's experience. 'Get out there and piss it in,' I told him. Well, Dye *didn't* piss it in. In fact, he and Prong O'Plenty got pissed *upon*. They came last by 10 lengths. I couldn't f**king believe it. I had prepared the Prong perfectly.

To save face, I had to find a scapegoat and I chose Shane Dye. The bastard had obviously taken no notice of my detailed riding instructions and his poor riding tactics were the reason for the embarrassing loss. As I do in any crisis, I acted decisively but fairly. I gave the skinny little prick a good going-over with his own whip right in front of the members stand.

With that fiasco out of the way, I hoped Prong O' Plenty would get his act together. But his best result in the next six outings was second last. What could I do? I asked Kris Lees around for a few beers and hoped he'd help me solve our problem. This time he didn't let me down. 'Prong looks a stayer. Let him run 2400 metres instead of 1200. Oh, and get him gelded.' It made sense, with that huge dick, he carried an extra 10 kilos every time he raced.

I took Kris's advice and entered the Prong in the following week's 2400-metre KB Cup at Randwick. I also made an appointment with the vet to get his cock cut off – yes, other trainers just get a horse's balls removed, but I'm not one for half measures.

The Prong was fine with the first bit of news but for some reason seemed much less enthusiastic about the second. 'Prong, old mate,' I pointed out to him, 'it's the sacrifice you have to make if you want to be great.' And I knew what I was talking about. I myself had been born with a set of grapefruit-sized testicles but when I became a teenager, as much as the sheilas loved my huge nuts, they did hamper my running style. I bit the bullet and had one temporarily removed (it's still at Mum and Dad's somewhere). From that moment on, I ran like the wind. 'Now,' I told the Prong, 'it's *your* turn.'

We headed off to the vet's but I was shocked to learn how expensive gelding is. When I informed the vet he was a f**king rip-off merchant, he laughed and told me to go and do the job myself. So I did, and it was a piece of cake. Two Aspro Clears, six Band-Aids and a butter knife, and the Prong's shagging days were officially over. After the operation he needed a new name, and it was an obvious choice. I rechristened him Prong O'Paltry. He didn't mind, he just loved to race.

Came the day of the KB Cup and I was bloody nervous. The race was an acid test. If Prong O' Paltry didn't respond to the longer distance or the loss of his dick and balls, my days as an owner–trainer were numbered.

I shouldn't have worried. The Prong jumped well and settled in just behind the leaders. It was clear to me that he was moving much better without his gargantuan member. He positioned himself nicely at the turn for home, then shot through. Taking the lead, he held off a late challenge to win the Cup.

Well, I went f**king hysterical. In my joy I groped everyone I could get my hands on. (Bart Cummings didn't seem to enjoy it too much, but you can't please everyone.) Then I made a beeline to the winner's circle to greet the Prong. I gave my boy a hug and a little tickle where his prick used to be, just to remind him not to get carried away. *I* was still the boss.

The Spring Carnival was now just seven weeks away, and I knew if we played our cards right, Prong O' Paltry could be going around on the first Tuesday in November. Some of our KB Cup winnings funded a little trip to the Gold Coast for the Prong and me. A bit of a drink and a freshen-up in the sun would do us both the world of good before heavy training kicked in again.

Most days we sat on the beach. I'd get shit-faced but I restricted Prong's intake to about four beers a day. Nights, I'd screw myself silly. More than once I looked across the hotel bedroom to where the now-prongless Prong was bunked and noticed an envious tear in his eye.

After our Gold Coast holiday, Prong and I returned to Newcastle and full training. We'd finish each day totally stuffed: Prong from the intense trackwork I put him through, me from sitting on my arse all day in the sun, drinking and barking orders. As a master tactician I'd calculated that if my horse was going to succeed as a stayer and regularly race over 2400–3000 metres I'd have to double his workload.

That meant hours of tearing down the highway and endless sandwork. Once I made him swim to Taree. Kris Lees warned me that I was burning the Prong out. This simply gave me the opportunity to tell Lees to f**k off, and I continued on my merry way.

By the time of the Spring Racing Carnival, Prong O'Paltry looked ripped and as hard as a rock. I was superconfident that by the end of the racing season we would both have made big names for ourselves, and become pretty bloody rich as well.

But bugger me if all the smartarse race experts didn't write off our chances of success. They reckoned I was too inexperienced as a trainer and the Prong was no better than a short-arsed plodder. I vowed to make them eat buckets of their own bullshit.

For the next few weeks, the Prong finished in the middle of the field in all the races we entered. Pundits continued to underestimate us, but I knew I was bringing him along well and that he'd be at his peak when it really mattered. I was enjoying my little game of ducks and drakes. When Damien Oliver rode the Prong to a fourth in the 3000-metre Geelong Cup I pretended to be disappointed, but in my head I was turning cartwheels.

The Caulfield Cup brought me back to earth with a thud. I told jockey Jimmy Cassidy to take the Prong to the front early and run 'em off their feet. Great plan, but when the gates opened, the Prong was scratching his arse and missed the kick by two lengths. At the finish, we'd made up lost ground and were only beaten by a short half head.

The critics took notice now. The Melbourne *Herald-Sun* ran the headline 'Bulgarian Wonderhorse Is Victorian Derby Favourite!'. In the derby, however, Cassidy rode a shocker. Prong O' Paltry looked tired and lacked zip throughout, and finished a god-awful 14th.

Hell hath no fury like a pissed-off Reg Reagan. I stormed onto the track and told Cassidy that if he ever dared to ride so badly again, I'd cut his dick off just like I cut off the Prong's. 'Shove it up your arse!' yelled Cassidy. At first I thought he was talking about his dick and I was a little taken aback, then I realised he was referring to my horse. No one talks to me like that. It was time to find a new jockey.

The Melbourne Cup was just days away when I found a young apprentice rider named Simon Marks, from Kembla Grange. He seemed a nice bloke and his girlfriend had a gorgeous arse.

The handicappers put 52 kilograms on our backs for the Cup and we drew the 3 barrier, a stroke of luck. To calm my nerves with the race just a couple of hours away, I got on the drink, and the combination of my hypertension and 47 schooners soon ensured that ol' Reggie was stone-cold legless. Not too pissed, however, to neglect to give my riding instructions to young Marks. 'Here's my genius plan,' I slurred. 'Go hard early, ease at two thousand metres, then let him go again at the turn for home!'

The jockey looked at me as if I came from the Planet Stupid, then said, 'Mr Reagan, your plan smells as bad as your breath!' He said a lot of other things as well. Basically, they boiled down to him refusing to follow my orders. As Marks ranted at me, I suddenly realised that as a revered owner–trainer I didn't have to debate a raving smartarse. So I wound up the conversation the Reg Reagan way. I hit Marks with a flurry of punches that left him lying in a bloody heap, his teeth sprayed all over his head like a *Star Wars* extra. Problem was, I'd maimed my jockey and shot myself in the foot.

With 10 minutes till the start, I had no choice. With the little soft cock in no condition to saddle up, I'd have to ride Prong O' Paltry in the Melbourne Cup myself. The problem was that the Prong was down to ride with 52 kilograms on his back and I weighed 102. Only my athletic prowess, big-game instincts and competitive know-how would get us through. The bookies were not convinced, however, and when the news came over the loudspeakers that I'd replaced Marks as jockey, the Prong's odds blew out from 33–1 to 150–1. That suited me just fine, and I gave a $50 note to a little princess and told her to get it on for me. I went through my riding plan one final time, then whispered in Prong O' Paltry's ear, 'Trust me, my prickless friend.'

The stewards gave the all clear to start and the light began to flash. I took a deep breath. The barriers flew open. I began to whip the Prong like a man possessed and rode him as hard as I had ever ridden. After only 1000 metres of the 3200-metre race, I was 20 lengths in front. I could hear the crowd laughing, but the jockeys eating my dust got nervous and started to give chase early. 'You little beauty,' I smirked. My plan was working perfectly.

With 1700 metres to go, I eased off the gas and just cruised, letting the others burn precious energy trying to catch us. This horse race was turning into a dogfight.

The pack had caught up as we made the turn for home. I could hear the other jockeys panting and swearing as they made their final bid to overtake the Prong and me. Now it was time to make these derelict dwarfs pay. Memories of Dallas Donnelly and Tommy Raudonikis flashed before my eyes. First Steven King, riding Jim's Pride, made his challenge, and as he thundered alongside on my right, he grinned at me as if to say, 'I've got your measure, Reg!' I wiped the smile from little Stevie's dial with a beautifully timed backhand whip to his ballbag. Jimmy Cassidy loomed up on my left. A problem, but nothing that a crack across his Adam's apple couldn't fix.

Looking back today at film footage of that race, I remind myself of a dominatrix in full flight, whipping the daylights out of those other riders and their mounts. In Kenny Calender's words, it was 'F**king Shuper Shtuff!'

About 200 metres from home, I gave the Prong one last whack and off he took like he had a rocket up his arse. With 100 metres to go I knew we were there. I greeted the judge Reagan-style with the old middle-finger salute.

All Flemington went crazy. 'Reg-gie! Reg-gie!' screamed the crowd. I acknowledged their acclaim by showing them my hairy arse. They loved me all the more.

But then, just as I was about to go berserk and start knocking back the grog and bedding sheilas in the stables, an announcement came over the PA system. In turn, the news was broadcast throughout the country on TV and radio. 'A protest for rough riding has been lodged against Prong O'Paltry and his rider, Reg Reagan!' Seems every one of the other jockeys in the race was mighty pissed off at us for our win-at-all-costs attitude. Watching in the medical bay as my fellow riders were stitched up and their concussions treated, the thought crossed my mind that they might have a point. Word got around that it would take a miracle for us to beat the protest and be named official winners of the Melbourne Cup.

I was called into the steward's room for the hearing. 'Oh, shit, I'm a goner,' I thought. Then, to my delight, I recognised the chief steward. He was an old mate from Griffith who had dated my sister Regan for a while. As I took my seat, he gave me a little wink. 'You f**king beauty!' I yelled.

My mate began the hearing by declaring that I'd been charged with bringing the Melbourne Cup into disrepute by beating the living crap out of the entire field, man and horse. 'How do you answer these charges?' he asked me.

'Hang on, mate,' I said. There was no way he was going to bamboozle me with high-falutin' legalese. 'What does "disrepute" mean?'

'It means turning the greatest horse race in the world into a bloody schemozzle, Reggie!'

I began to weep (fake tears, of course, Reg Reagan *never* cries). 'Well, your Honour, what else could I do? I had to win. I have so many mouths at home to feed . . . and there's my foster child in Zambia I'm trying to keep from starving . . .'

'We sympathise, but your behaviour on the track today was pretty extreme, mate.'

Through my crocodile tears, I gathered steam. 'If you disqualify me, the ones who'll suffer most are the 30 or more charities I was going to give my prize money to. Rub me out, and it'll be on your conscience.'

'Then name those charities,' demanded the steward.

'Errr . . .'

Shane Dye piped up. 'This is an outrage,' he yelled.

I leapt to my feet. 'The only outrageous thing here is your hair, pin dick!'

The steward banged his hand on the bench. 'Order! Now, Reg, what is the name of at least one of the charities you support?'

'The Melbourne Racing Club,' I said.

'Oh, gee whiz,' replied the chief steward, growing calmer now. 'Jolly good show, Reggie Boy.'

'Look, sure,' I continued, 'I belted a few of these super-sensitive little prima donnas, but isn't it about time someone dragged 'em into line? Take you stewards, you guys – or heroes, as I like to call ya – work your arses off each year for next to nothing. All you blokes get is abuse and the back-hand of an ugly sheila you call your wife. Don't deny it, boys, I've seen 'em. Meanwhile, these little jockey tarts travel the world, earn shitloads and get roots you stewards don't dare even wank over. So, you guys tell me, protest upheld, or protest thrown out?' The room fell deathly quiet for a few long, cold seconds.

'Case dismissed!' chorused the officials. 'You've won the Melbourne Cup!'

And that's why to this day my name is up there with T J Smith, Bart Cummings, George Moore and Johnny Tapp in the pantheon of Australian horse racing. As an owner, trainer and jockey, no one did it better than old Reg Reagan in his prime.

Prong O'Paltry? Well, I hate to say it, but Kris Lees was right. I burned the Prong out in less than a year and tricked a bunch of towelheads from Dubai into buying him for a few million dollars as a stud horse. Imagine their surprise when they had a closer look between his legs.

I wish I could say I'm a wealthy man today because of my great foray into racing. But I can't. I spent some of my winnings on fast women, some on slow horses . . . and I wasted some of it, too.

20

A MAN AMONG MEN

I'VE BEEN THROUGH SO MUCH in my life, and I can say my trials and tribulations have made me what I am today. Extremely bitter.

But no, most people when they reach my age are ready to put their feet up and take it easy. Not me. I'm always looking for the next challenge, another triumph. If you'd had a life of outstanding achievement like mine, you'd understand that I find it impossible to settle for second best. All things considered, I'd say old Reggie Reagan in his golden years is busier than at any other period in his life. So, I thought I'd give all my fans who'll never know greatness a little reminder of the heavy demands that my celebrity lumbers me with.

Deputy Chief CEO of the National Rugby League

This is a role I generally like to keep secret from the media

Imagine my surprise when after a typical Les and Tommy Mad Monday piss-up, I woke up at the top of Everest.

and the general public. I prefer to let the likes of David Gallop enjoy their moment in the sun while it lasts.

As the NRL's deputy chief CEO I assist Gallop and his board in all aspects of decision-making. For instance, I'm proud to be able to reveal that it was yours truly who decided to give Billy Idol the 2002 Grand Final gig. Idol's performance is still being talked about to this day.

Not that the NRL board and I always agree. Right now we're having a bit of a blue. I want to dump the Hoodoo Gurus' 'That's My Team' promotion and replace the band with a true international superstar kids can relate to. Someone like, say, Boy George or Adam Ant.

I'm always pushing for progress in the game. I realise that we are constantly in competition with other sports for the fans' support and the sponsors' bucks. For this reason, last year I came up with a few subtle rule changes, which the board is currently considering. Here are just a few of my revolutionary ideas:

- Points to be awarded to teams for defence, as well as when they score a try or kick a goal. You get one point for a tackle around the legs, two points for an above-the-waist tackle, eight points for a solid tackle above the neck. You score a bonus point if the victim is sent to the blood bin.
- A 'white horse system' where, if a team is kept to zero, every player must dispose of their shorts and underwear (if they're wearing any) and run 10 laps of the field holding hands and singing the opposing team's victory song.
- A new sin-bin set-up, because I've found that players no longer fear the existing one. If a player is sent to the sin bin for 10 minutes he will be taken into the dressing room, handcuffed to a locker and buggerised by the

opposition coach and/or team manager. Then he is allowed to return to the field of play.
- Let the TV cameras into the dressing rooms more often. Little innovations such as a hidden camera under the soap holders in the showers would take away a lot of the guesswork, giving viewers at home insight into just who are our great game's real men and who are the soft cocks.

I'm confident that all my innovations will come into effect by the start of the 2005 season and that Rugby League will be an even greater game as a direct result.

Music Mogul

I am currently employed, at a huge salary, to be an adviser to Sony Music. Therefore, I'm always on the lookout for talent. But what you all have to understand is that the music industry is not just about the music any more. It's about the 'look', and having a nice, clean, healthy, responsible image. I can reveal that on my recommendation Sony very soon will be making a big play to sign up Courtney Love. I can also take credit for Sony signing George Michael.

I'm obviously the man for the job. I've got a few No. 1 singles and albums to my name, sold out Wembley with The Reg Reagan Band and am a true legend of rock. I really love my music, although that wasn't always so. For a time when I was young I thought pop and rock were the work of the devil. I can thank Cyndi Lauper for turning me on to music. It was in the early '80s I started dating Cyndi, and I caught the music bug from her. We co-wrote 'Girls Just Wanna Have Fun', although the title I suggested was 'Girls Just Wanna Have Sex'. Her Mr Know-It-All agent decided it was in bad taste.

Friend To All

Mates are very important to me, and keeping in touch with all my friends takes up a lot of my time. There's nothing old Reg relishes more than going down to the pub with a few of his closest mates, whacking a few songs on the jukebox and tearing into the piss. A few of the blokes try to get lucky with the birds there, but yours truly only tries it on occasionally these days. As you may have noticed I've stacked on a little weight, in all the sexiest places, of course. My wedding band refuses to slip off my finger any more, and I'm discovering that, unlike before, sheilas are reluctant to experiment with a married man.

Tragedy struck my close circle of mates recently when good old Slippery Steve died in an unfortunate accident. Steve was a real character in his day, and probably the biggest show pony God ever put breath into. He was into body building, and even in winter would strut around Cessnock in little more than a pair of Speedos. But the birds loved Steve, and his penchant for lairing up extended even to him attaching mirrors to his bedroom ceiling so he could watch himself shag. Karma got Steve in the end. One night while he was engaging in a bit of one-handed action, the mirrors came loose from their screws, fell onto our dear friend and cut him up into small pieces. All the boys chipped in and bought him the best headstone in the local cemetery. On the front we inscribed: 'Here Lies Slippery Steve, A Man Who Literally Loved Himself To Death'.

Sports Critic

Even though sport is not the turn-on it was in the days when I was a champion, I spend many hours a day watching it on television. Whether cricket, Rugby League or synchronised swimming, I'll sit glued to the box, a pie in one hand, an icy cold KB in the other, and a neighbour's wife on my lap.

One thing that does get right up my nose, however, is when these 'stars' of today get put on a pedestal by fans and the media. It irks me when I see them big-noting themselves day in and day out, when I know very well that even at my age I could be out there doing a shitload better job than the lot of 'em. Here are a few of the overrated imposters . . .

Andrew Johns: Many people marvel at Johns's skills. The only thing I marvel at is the size of his arse. I shared so much of my football knowledge with this kid back in my Newcastle Knights days, but has he ever given me due credit in public? No chance. Put Johns in front of a microphone and he seems to get f**king amnesia about the bloke who's made him what he is today. I hope he gets as much satisfaction looking at his Dally M Medals and Golden Boots as I get looking at him being smashed every week.

Gorden Tallis: Let me get straight to the point. Big Gordo wouldn't have lasted two minutes with me when I was in my prime. I was faster, stronger and bigger. But I have a soft spot for the kid. It must be the way he shakes and quivers whenever he's in my company: a mixture of hero worship and being intimidated. The Raging Bull? Back in the glorious '70s he'd have been branded the Raging Homo!

Nathan Hindmarsh: I love this kid from the Parramatta Eels, I really do. He looks like a rootin' tootin' straight-shootin' country bumpkin, who couldn't give a shit. But, son, take a look at how you wear your shorts. They dangle down around your f**kin' knees. Now, I'm pretty liberal, and

I don't mind staring at a bloke's arse (back in my navy days I thrived on it), but fair dinkum, enough's enough. I get sick of turning on my Friday night footy on Channel Nine and having Nathan Hindmarsh's hairy arse jammed down my throat. Jesus, that's what SBS is for.

Son, I have a solution that I think we can all benefit from. Back when I was murdering 'em on the field week in, week out, I actually went the other way and pulled my footy shorts up nice and high. They were cut bloody tight too. In fact, you could see the veins in my balls. After the game I'd be swamped by sheilas and shirt-lifters alike. Hindmarsh, think about following my example. I'd appreciate it, and so will truckloads of groupies, I promise.

Jason Stevens: C'mon, big guy. Let's loosen the shoulders a little bit and start getting down and dirty with the ladies. I mean, take a look at him. He's a chick magnet, a bloke who has it all. He's a gentleman and he has those brooding Mediterranean looks. He dresses well. Get him on the field and he loves to rip in. Who could forget the time he stamped on that pommy bastard's face? Brilliant!

I like the bloke and offer him advice whenever I can. I appreciate the fact that he's saving himself for marriage because of his religious beliefs, but, gee whiz, if I was a woman I'd think his decision to abstain from sex till he's married was mighty selfish. Stevo and I are very similar blokes. I, too, am deeply religious. The only difference is that my god encourages me to drink and demands that I bang as many sheilas as possible. But, as my old man used to say, 'Reg, a man has only his convictions,' so, in keeping with that good advice I want to go on record as saying that I support Jason in whatever he chooses to do. I just hope I'm there hiding in his bedroom wardrobe the night his long wait ends. I reckon it'll be like a fire hydrant going off.

Matthew Hayden and **Justin Langer**: I'll grant these fellas this: they are very good cricketers. But what about the way they carry on when they get a century opening stand? All this kissing and hugging and shit! Jesus, it makes me want to spew.

I can remember the days of real cricketers, and I know for a fact you'd never catch Phil Tufnell or Greg Matthews carrying on this way.

Jonny Wilkinson: Looks like a choirboy. Plays like one, too. People wax lyrical about this pommy bastard's goal kicking, but anyone lucky enough to have seen *me* kick goals would know this bloke isn't fit to wipe my hairy arse.

And another thing: the peculiar kicking stance that has made him so famous? I was doing it way back when I was playing for Woy Woy. I might also add that I whacked a copyright on the style and am looking forward to dragging his pretty-boy arse right through our corrupt court system.

Harry Kewell: Harry was coming through the ranks at Leeds while I was enjoying my illustrious Manchester United experience. He was only in his teens then, and he nearly drove me crazy with his hero worship. He followed me around to the point of stalking, and a few times I was forced to threaten the little bastard with an AVO if he didn't leave me alone.

Kewell's persistence paid off, however, and I spent a fair portion of my time showing him how to play the game of soccer. He was a very nice young man, but has changed since he started earning mega-dollars and married a soap star. It's a shame that, like Andrew Johns, he has forgotten all about the bloke who pointed him to the top. A few bucks and a night out with one of his missus's friends would be nice but to date all I've received from the ungrateful little bastard is an autographed photograph that states: 'To Reg, who the f**k are you! Harry.'

Kostya Tszyu: Now, here's a bloke who really pisses me off. I remember an incident one night at South Sydney Leagues Club just after Tszyu came to Australia from Russia. I bumped into him and happened to ask how he was enjoying his adopted homeland. He replied, 'Sorry, don't understand.'

That got my back up. 'Here,' I said, 'let me explain myself more clearly,' and I hit the Siberian so-called tough guy with a left to the guts. Tszyu fell to his knees while one of his security men, who obviously had a violence problem, belted me over the back of the head, knocking me senseless. For six months I had a lump on my scone the size of a rockmelon, which served as a painful reminder of the savage and unprovoked attack. More than once since, I've dared Tszyu to face me man-to-man in the ring but he continues to ignore my challenges.

And he has added insult to injury by stating in the media that I am nothing but a 'smelly, dirty, cowardly alcoholic yobbo who is stuck in the '70s'. Yeah, well, Tzsyu, so what if I do smell? So what if I only tub once or twice a year? Am I an alcoholic? F**kin' oath! A coward? Well, pigtail-boy, get in the ring with me and find out. I guarantee you'll wish you were back eating sardines outside your igloo.

Rugby Union: I don't understand the so-called game they play in heaven. To me, Rugby resembles some kind of weird medieval gay orgy. Every time a bloke hits the deck he's jumped on by dozens of sweaty blokes who look like they're trying to get their rocks off. I'm sure it's very erotic for rugger-buggers but I reckon it makes for shithouse television.

Having said that, I've a soft spot for Australian skipper Georgie Gregan. I love the way the cheeky prick delights in wandering around the paddock for 80 minutes not doing too much more than making an arsehole of himself. He hates refs nearly as much as I did and he should be commended for keeping the cheating bastards honest. I've been shocked and horrified over the past few years to see his abrasive style of captaincy questioned and criticised. I mean, fair dinkum, what are we looking for in our leaders, a bloke who'll slip off to the ref's change room before the match and slip him a hummer just so the 50–50 decisions go his team's way? Well, shove that up your arse. We'll leave that sort of stuff to the pommies.

Australian Rules: While strictly a ladies' man, I must say I'm impressed by the tightness of AFL players' shorts and guernseys. These blokes have got their heads screwed on right. They know that through the magnificent medium that is television, millions of women have the opportunity to size up the dimensions of a bloke's 'cut lunch' while admiring his ball skills. I mean, as a spectacle the sport is a complete joke, but it does have that hunk factor that, after my retirement, went missing from Rugby League.

Take Warwick Capper – now, there's a smart bloke. As a footballer he could barely kick a cow in the guts and, let's be honest, if you dressed him in a three-piece suit, sheilas wouldn't give him a second glance. Yet, Warwick overcame all his shortcomings to become one of Australian sport's greatest sex symbols through the 1980s. How did he do it? By winning Brownlow Medals? No. By starring in grand finals? No. By having a handsome melon? Get real! He achieved his popularity by slipping on a pair of red shorts so tight you could see the pulse in his gonads.

When Warwick and I hit the town together back in the '80s, the sheilas couldn't keep their hands off him. Admittedly, sitting there at the bar with yours truly did his charisma factor no harm, but I can't take all the credit. That's got to go to the way he packed his red shorts. Yes, Warwick was probably the first athlete of his kind. A bloke who had a mile of front and wasn't afraid to use it.

These days Aussie Rules misses blokes like Warwick Capper. Now, sadly, shorts are looser and baggier. Why? Smartarses are saying that bigger shorts are more comfortable and improve performance on the field. Well, boys, I'll take a painted-on pair of scrotum huggers and female admiration any time.

High Fashion Guru

I was pretty good mates with Gianni Versace. We met about 15 years ago at the opening of a Target store in Mudgee. Gianni and I hit it off straight away, and every now and then in the years before his tragic murder we made an effort to catch up. He invited me to go to Milan for a reunion one summer. He also offered me a fortune to whip up a few threads and model them at one of his big men's fashion shows. I jumped at the chance, even though I was pretty nervous. I mean, I'm a pretty snappy dresser, everyone knows that, but creating my own designs and strutting down the catwalk in front of a thousand or so wogs was slightly daunting.

Turned out the show was a huge success. The crowd

marvelled at my body-hugging black shirts, scrotum-revealing shorts, and leather-look accessories. *Milan Modelling World* magazine described my presentation as 'strangely feral but heartwarming'. After that, Gianni got me on board and I did many magazine shoots for him.

When news came through that my dear friend had been shot dead, I was shattered – shattered on the piss, that is. It wasn't till I sobered up three days later that the tragedy really sank in. I jumped on a plane to Milan to comfort Gianni's grieving family. It was a very emotional time. I'm proud to say that Gianni's sister, Donatella, still visits us in Cessnock and phones me most days. I give her little tips here and there on where I believe fashion is headed. Least I can do. Think about it, now. Have a guess who kicked off the ugh boot craze all over again? As we say in Milan, *moi*.

High fashion runs in the Reagan family. I'm pleased to report that my son, Rick, is interested in a catwalk career, which makes me proud, even though I worry that he's got a bit of shirt-lifter in him.

Womaniser

I'm many things, but a pillow-biter I'm not. I love women, immensely. I enjoy their company, particularly in the fart sack. And women seem to love me as well, which has caused more than a few problems with the missus over the years. No matter where I go, the media is always linking me with one bird or another. Like the time in England when the local tabloids had a field day talking up my so-called affair with Sarah Ferguson, the Duchess of York. To this day, people still hound me, wanting to know if the reports were fact or fiction. One of my policies is to treat women with respect, so that definitely means no kiss and tell from yours truly. Sure, I spent time with Fergie; sure, we were good friends; sure, I was quoted in the *News of the World* that she was for certain a natural redhead; but, apart from that, my lips are sealed.

While in Paris visiting some old friends at Fashion Week, I was linked to just about every supermodel who ever paraded down a catwalk. My Ruthie called me in the Hotel de Crillon one morning after images of me swimming naked in the hotel pool with Elle Macpherson, Naomi Campbell and Heidi Klum were splashed all over the papers back home. Fair dinkum, those paparazzi couldn't have had much to do that night.

Claudia Schiffer really had the hots for old Reggie and I had a soft spot for her too. Unfortunately, she was dating that arsewipe magician David Copperfield at the time. The dickhead could make elephants vanish without a trace but he could never quite make *himself* disappear, and constantly cramped Claudia's and my style. Probably just as well – with the wife at home, I was only going to get myself into trouble.

I've dated hundreds of beautiful women over the years but have always treated them with the respect they deserve. My old man, Ray, taught me a code of ethics and I've stuck by it:

- Never raise your voice to a woman (unless it's during orgasm).
- Never swear in front of a woman (unless you're asking her for a f**k).
- Never have sex with a woman on the first date (unless she's above seven out of 10).
- After sex, always insist on calling a taxi for the woman so she can go home.

- Never French-kiss a woman who has hairy feet, a deeper voice than John Laws and an Adam's apple.

Each Christmas I call up many of my old girlfriends and invite them around for a barbecue to catch up. Ruthie gets a bit paranoid about it all, but so long as she doesn't catch me getting a blow job or fondling their tits, she doesn't seem to mind too much.

Anti-Drug Crusader

Drugs are the scourge of the friggin' earth! I tell any youngsters I see that if they want a one-way ticket to an early grave, get on the drugs.

I'd love to come out and say that I never touched 'em, but I can't. I'm no cleanskin. In my surfing days I experimented a little with ganga, and at different times in my life I became addicted to Aspro Clear, Sudafed – and even to heavier stuff, like musk Lifesavers.

I can't stress it enough: if you are offered drugs, please say no! Apart from the health aspect, the person doing the offering might be an undercover cop.

Demon Drinker

My dad, Ray, introduced me to alcohol before a school dance when I was 13, and we've been tight ever since.

Booze has been a true friend that's stuck with me through thick and thin, unlike many women and fair-weather friends. No matter if a relationship has broken up, a close mate has died, or it's half-time in a tight game, the taste of the golden nectar soothes my soul and reminds me everything will be all right.

My drink of choice is beer, and my beer of choice is KB. Having said that, I'll drink goat's piss if I think it'll get me drunk. I've sat and shared a cleansing ale with kings, queens, movie stars, sporting champions, prime ministers and barflies. But nothing beats sitting in the Aussie sun, turning a banger on the barbie with a group of close mates, baggin' someone behind their back and enjoying an ice-cold KB. That'll do me, folks, that's heaven.

State of Origin Trainer (and Coach)

In 2003, New South Wales coach Phil Gould invited me to oversee the training of his State of Origin team. I agreed but early on had reservations. To me the blokes selected seemed a motley crew of pretty boys and no-hopers. But in no time at all, in a fashion that surprised even me, I whipped the lads into a finely tuned, enormously fit bunch of elite athletes.

There's been plenty of speculation since we flogged Queensland in the series that I was actually the coach of the team and Gould was purely the front man. Look, I won't confirm or deny that sort of crap, but if I had to I'd probably lean towards confirming it. Anyway, I was more than comfortable being the man in the shadows, particularly if one of the young single blokes brought a sheila into the camp.

A lot was made of the supposed 'rift' between Phil Gould and Joey Johns. Photos appeared on the front and back pages of the newspapers showing them in a 'heated exchange'. I can say right now that there was no heated exchange. In fact, there was no exchange at all. Gould and Johns didn't talk to each other at any stage in the campaign and it was left to me to mediate constantly between the two by means of written notes and hand signals. To both Gould and Johns's credit, however, they got on with the job and didn't let their problems affect the side.

The bonding sessions were pretty special and I got enormous pleasure out of drinking some so-called stars under the table, sometimes on the morning of the game. These sessions were the secret to our tight-knit unity. Fair dinkum, I've never seen a group of blokes bond together better. Apart from Ricketson, Johns, Buderus, Minichiello, Bailey, Timmins, Ryles and Fletcher, all the boys got on great and had tremendous respect for each other.

The coaching staff was a key ingredient too. The brains trust of Gould, Laurie 'Lozza' Daley and my good self spent endless hours in front of the video recorder watching pornographic movies and 1980s' Queensland games, always looking for something that would give our boys that little edge.

After we'd wrapped up the series in Game II, Gus and Lozza came up, threw their arms around me and said, 'Reggie, we couldn't have done it without ya.' It was a shame the feeling wasn't mutual.

Origin is very special. It conjures up unique emotions. Only the very fit and mentally tough survive. I really enjoyed the experience and even now I'm stewing over whether to take on the job again. Last year I found it hard to fit my many State of Origin commitments into my schedule. I found myself rushing to and fro between Paris, Milan, Sydney and Brisbane. The offer to hitch up with the Blues again is one I take seriously and I'm acutely aware that Origin will not be the same without me. But there comes a time when one must put oneself first.

The hardest thing will be not being part of the squad, not being there when the boys are on the grog or running and spewing their guts up on the training paddock. I'll also miss the victory song after the wins, especially since I wrote the f**kin' thing in a moment of pure inspiration. Seeing the fellas belting it out never failed to bring tears to my eyes. Written to the tune of 'Simply the Best', it went like this: 'We're simply the best/Tougher than a plastic breast/Better than anyone/Particularly in the love nest.' You repeat it 12 times, then finish it off with 'You f**kin' beauty!' It was surprising it only reached No. 3 in the ARIA charts.

Guardian of Australian Values

I'll be honest. I'm bloody nervous about Australia's future. I believe we are being corrupted by dangerous foreign forces and that the very essence of what it means to be Australian is disappearing. Take the Aussie language, for instance. These days, I hear young Australian blokes referring to a sheila's tit as 'a lady's breast'. That's not Aussie talk, friends, that's poof talk. There are many other examples of how our great language has gone to seed. In my day we called the male reproductive organ the 'cock', the 'schlong', the 'stag', the 'salami', or even the 'prick'. Nowadays, kids are calling it the 'penis'. To me, that word sounds so sterile. No wonder young blokes are struggling to get laid!

Which brings me to my next point. I am shocked and horrified to hear the likes of Rugby League footballer Jason Stevens and that frizzy haired *Australian Idol* winner Guy Sebastian saying they're virgins and are 'saving themselves' for marriage. *Heavens a-bloody-bove!* Back when I was in primary school, any kid who was a virgin was the laughing stock of the playground. We'd lie about our sexual conquests to save ourselves the embarrassment of getting a reputation as a sexual greenhorn. In fact, back in third class I was known as 'Root-a-Day-Reg'. My old man wouldn't let me in the house after school if he suspected I'd abstained from sex that day. How times have changed. Today these virgins are friggin' heroes. I tell you, I'm confused. Where in the Bible does it state, 'Thou shalt not enjoy a bit of nookie'? I rest my case.

In my humble opinion, Australian society started on its sharp downhill spiral when they got rid of the Sydney Cricket Ground Hill and replaced it with a cold concrete grandstand that harbours shirt-lifters and pricks in suits. I used to love nothing more than sitting on the old Hill, and whenever I scored a try at the SCG during my fabulous Rugby League career I always made sure I saluted the hallowed mound. The Hill had everything: beer cans, Pluto Pups, sheilas in bikinis and the sweet smell of a bit of hoochy-kootch being passed around. When I heard they were going to get rid of the Hill, I protested to the wankers on the SCG Trust. They replied that the new stand 'was simply what the public wanted'. What we *wanted*! What we *wanted*! I didn't want it and neither did any of my mates! Maybe a few asylum seekers wanted a new grandstand, but who gives a shit about them? Fair dinkum, are we living in Australia or friggin' Eastern Europe?

And whatever happened to good old Aussie tucker? I'll tell you. It's being phased out and replaced by foreign fancy-pants food. I was dragged to a restaurant the other night to celebrate young Reg Jnr's girlfriend's 21st birthday. I looked at the menu and couldn't believe my eyes. Here I was, in Australia, and all I was being offered was stir-fries, pasta and bloody risotto. Being a gentle soul and not wanting to cause a scene, I discreetly summoned the waiter and inquired, 'Where are the f**kin' Chiko Rolls and the egg and bacon sandwiches?' Well, the rude pony-tailed prick rolled his eyes and laughed at me. Right up until I collared him and used his face for an appetiser. Nope, you can have your Chinese, Japanese, Italian, Lebanese, Greek and French cuisine. Give me a pie and a sausage roll or light up the barbie, and as far as old Reg is concerned, you're cooking with gas.

Olympics Inspiration

The 2000 Games were a big occasion for me. Not only was I a consultant to the Aussie team but I was an Olympic official, and when Graham Richardson became ill, I filled in as mayor of the Olympic Village. It was so rewarding to work closely with the athletes. I enjoyed sharing their highs and lows. Particularly their lows.

Being there for Cathy Freeman was very rewarding. She was as nervous as shit before her 400 metres semifinal and final, and to see her receive her gold medal and know I had been an integral part of her triumph warmed the cockles of my heart. Before the final, Cathy had approached me and asked how she should attack her race. My message was simple: 'Get out of the blocks and run like hell!' The whole world now knows that she followed my advice, doing exactly that.

I also encouraged her to wear a full bodysuit I had designed for her. She did that, too. Sure, she looked ridiculous, but dear Lord, it was effective. The bodysuit was an innovation I kicked off when I was playing Rugby League for the Young Cherrypickers. The winters down that way are extremely cold and I wore the bodysuit to combat the freezing conditions. After a while, I began to understand the aerodynamics the suit created and that whenever I wore the suit in a game I was untouchable. Sorry, let me rephrase that, even *more* untouchable. I gave the tip to Cathy years later and the rest is history. Cathy begged me to accept her gold medal as a token of her appreciation but, of course, I refused.

Another athlete I took great joy in being involved with back in 2000 was 'Jumpin'' Jai Taurima, who won a silver medal in the long jump. Now, Jai is renowned for being a beer-loving, nicotine-inhaling, pizza-eating, Superman-tattooed kind of guy. He's something of a rebel in world athletics. This wasn't always the case. When I first met Jai in 1998, he was painfully shy and in the grip of a trainer whose strict methods were squeezing the lifeblood out of the kid. He was on a diet consisting of not much more than birdseed. The Australian Institute of Sport called me one day and asked for help in turning Jai's life and career around. He had decided to quit elite sport because he was so miserable, and the AIS was keen to keep him on track for the Sydney Games.

I assured Jai that with Reg Reagan as his trainer, life was about to get a whole lot more fun. We drank piss till dawn every night, ate every kind of deep-fried food known to man, and smoked full-strength cigarettes till our fingers and teeth were yellow. And training? 'F**k training!' was our motto. Sure, we went to the track, but only to laugh at the other athletes busting their guts. By the time the Olympics came around, Jai's body looked a disgrace, but mentally the kid was ready.

On the day of his event, Jai asked me what his tactics should be. I told him, 'Go out there, son, with a smile on your face, your heart on your sleeve and blood in your donger, and you're sure to be a winner.' Jai revving up the crowd and launching into his jumps with the look of a kid loving life and with nothing to lose remains one of the great memories of Sydney 2000.

Well, we nearly pulled off a miracle. Jai would have got gold except for an arsey last jump from that communist Cuban prick. Still, Jai was weeping tears of joy on the dais as he received his silver medal. When he climbed down, he made a beeline for me and put his medal around my neck. 'Reggie, this was all your work. I love ya, mate.' I almost gave it back but then realised he was right. My only regret is that it wasn't gold. Who knows what I would have got for it at Cash Converters.

I have to admit that the 2000 Sydney Olympics wasn't all glory for me. I found myself embroiled in controversy when I was officiating during the 20,000-metres women's walk. My job was to check that the walkers were not lifting their feet or walking in an incorrect way when they entered Stadium Australia. My instructions were that if I saw anyone flouting the rules I had to raise my red card and disqualify them. It was a stinking hot day and I'd really given the KBs a nudge, and I guess I might have been a little disoriented when Aussie girl Jane Saville rounded a bend way ahead of the pack and headed towards the stadium and the finish line. She was a gold medal certainty.

Now, the 20,000-metre walk is my wife Ruth's favourite event, so I thought it would be a nice gesture if I got Jane Saville's autograph. Problem was, I had nothing for her to sign except the red card. Not wanting to cause a fuss I strolled up to Jane and discreetly shoved the card in her face, hoping she'd sign it for me. All of a sudden, hell broke loose. The head official was screaming: 'Disqualification!

Disqualification!' Jane was in floods of tears. I was public enemy No. 1. TV cameras were thrust in my face and reporters were demanding to know why I'd tossed Jane out of the race. I had to think fast. I couldn't say it had all been a mistake and I was after her signature. So, I explained that I had no choice but to disqualify her because, to my trained official's eye, her left hipbone was not properly aligned with her big toe.

Jane was understandably pissed off at me, but after I took her out for a few cold ones, she accepted my apology. She was such a good sport that she even gave me the autograph for Ruth, but I threw it away. I mean, who wants the signature of someone who's been disqualified?

All in all, the Sydney Olympics were a marvellous experience for me and I'm looking forward to making my mark in Athens.

GLOBETROTTER

While I enjoy travelling and soaking up the many varied cultures of pubs across the nation, I must admit that overseas travel doesn't interest me as much as it used to. I find the long flights tiring, everything too expensive and foreigners generally stupid. I've been to the world's most renowned landmarks and, to be perfectly honest, I found them boring.

Take the Eiffel Tower. It's a big steel erection crawling with smelly little Frenchmen. But Paris intrigues me. It's as if God rounded up the greatest arseholes on the planet and stuck them in a single city. What baffles me is that my family tree has roots in Paris, the nastiest, most up-itself joint on earth, and we're all so mild-mannered and easygoing.

The Great Wall of China was anything but great! There

were bloody Asians everywhere. It was like the Gold Coast without a beach. Walking the length of this decrepit eyesore gave me an enormous thirst, but do you reckon I could get a cold beer get anywhere? Not a chance! If any of you are contemplating visiting the wall, heed my advice. Take your own piss and a spray can. A bit of graffiti would liven up the useless pile of rocks.

Like nearly every bastard in the street these days, I've climbed Mount Everest. When you read about the legendary mountain, they always rattle on about action, adventure and excitement. Well, let me break the news to you, this is bullshit. The place is so isolated and primitive that there's nothing to do but climb to the top, take a quick look around, then piss off back down. Everest has no nightclubs or bars of any kind, and the weather is shithouse. The locals are so wrapped up in thick woolly skins you can't tell the blokes from the sheilas. Think Bangkok without bikinis. No, if you're after a holiday of fun, frivolity and the odd stray root, Everest is definitely overrated.

A few mates and I once visited the game parks of South Africa. We managed to sneak our various weapons through customs, only to find that the national parks authorities there ban tourists from using guns. So there we were with our Russian AK-47 automatic rifles and bazookas, and those South African pricks in safari suits wouldn't let us use them . . . at least, not on animals. They told us we had to do the 'tourist thing' and ride around on the back of a bus, viewing the lions, rhinos, tigers and elephants from a f**kin' mile away. Luckily, I managed to smuggle a small handgun onboard and was able to take down a few endangered species while our guide wasn't looking.

I've done Rome several times, and visited the Vatican. People rave about this place, but to me the Vatican is just a heap of religious mumbo jumbo. Even the paintings on the ceiling of the Sistine Chapel, by some bloke named Michelangelo, had me shaking my head. They were crap. Fair dinkum, give a wog a paintbrush and he thinks he's a genius. I'll take Ken Done any day. While I was in Rome I dropped into the Colosseum, made famous by Russell Crowe in *Gladiator*. This place may have a history, but the facilities were drastically outdated. Quite frankly, it doesn't compare to Aussie Stadium.

Italy is also renowned for its opera. People say they find it so moving it reduces them to tears. Well, it certainly moved me. I walked out of the theatre 15 minutes after the curtains opened. They didn't sing a single word of English. No thank you, very much. Give me AC/DC, John Farnham and Holly Valance.

By now you'll be noticing a trend here, people. Don't be fooled into spending big bucks on flashy foreign holidays. Everything you need is right here at home, in Australia. Want an example? Go visit Cessnock and, no, I don't mean the bloody vineyards. Take in the real 'Nock' by having a beer at the leagues club, or crack a few at Peden's Hotel. Maybe even don the black and gold, and cheer on the Goannas Rugby League team on a Sunday arvo. I guarantee Cessnock Sportsground makes the Colosseum look like the public toilet it is.

Or why not visit Bathurst and drive around the famous mountain that made us all fall in love with motorsport? You can have Mount Everest and Sir Edmund Hillary, I'll take Mount Panorama and Peter Brock.

If it's a sex tour you're after, forget about the bloody

Philippines, where the food is shit and the beaches smell. Pay a visit instead to Brisbane's Fortitude Valley. It's reasonably priced and just a stone's throw from the statue of Wally Lewis at Suncorp Stadium. Florence can stick its statue of David right up its arse. We have the *real* king.

Want culture? Don't even think about wasting your bucks on pricey journeys to the Louvre in Paris or to Madrid's Prado. Sure, they've got paintings and artefacts that date back to Biblical times, but if you want to get the buzz Warney does when he takes '5 for', check out the treasures on display at Sydney's very own Powerhouse Museum. There you can see Billy Thorpe's guitar and a Bee Gees' toupee. And you won't find any shirt-lifters, either, just good, clean ridgey-didge fun.

Reg Reagan loves this bloody country, and unless someone else is paying, there's no need to leave our you-beaut shores anytime soon. But if you do, let me pass on a few travel tips I've learned in a lifetime of globetrotting . . .

- Take the time to learn the local customs. This can save you embarrassment. For instance, who'd know that in Bangkok the prostitutes regard it as rude if you attempt to pay prior to orgasm, or that in Auckland it's legal to murder someone who utters the words 'Trevor Chappell'.
- Humour is a great icebreaker the world over. For instance, when visiting the Middle East, painting the American flag on a mate's backpack always gets the locals laughing.
- It's difficult and boring, but before you set off, try to learn at least a few of the local words. People will appreciate the effort you've made, even though the language is almost impossible in some places, like Russia, China and New Zealand.

Try to have an interpreter handy in case of an emergency. I remember a certain trip to India. I was in a restaurant in Bombay and ordered lamb vindaloo. The dish was so spicy it just about blew my head off my shoulders. There was me trying to explain in English to the curry-munching waiter that my tongue was on fire and I needed a cold beer quick-smart. The bloke didn't have a clue what I was on about, so, in a desperate attempt to show him that the vindaloo was way too hot, I dropped my pants, spread my cheeks and showed him my arsehole, which was bright red and weeping. Next thing, the police arrived and charged me with trying to seduce the waiter.

- Learn a thing or two about the country you're visiting. This can kick-start a conversation with locals in a bar or restaurant, and lead to friendships. For instance, when in Brazil talk soccer, and in Germany, be sure to remind the locals of Hitler.
- Let people know you're Australian. We have an excellent reputation abroad, thanks to friendly, good-humoured and easygoing blokes like Steve Irwin, Maxie Walker and David Hicks.

21
THIS WAS MY LIFE

STANDING THERE ON STAGE in Studio 9 I was nearing the end of my story. I looked out through the lights, past Mike Munro, and the *This Is Your Life* studio audience, at the cameras that crowded in on me transmitting my epic life journey to millions of viewers nationwide. What I saw going on around me was, in a word, f**kin' chaos.

It seemed like half the invited guests were being restrained by Channel Nine security guards from storming onto the stage and tearing me apart. Their faces were contorted with hatred. I can only assume they were pissed off by my honest portrayal of them and my warts-and-all retelling of what happened when our paths crossed. My old man, Ray, was drunk and angry as hell. 'Son,' he screamed at me, 'you've f**ked my credibility. I'm the laughing stock of Australia!' I felt sorry for the old fella, but honestly, his credibility had taken a ride up shit creek years ago, and I took his ungrateful outburst with a grain of salt.

A lot of the old tarts I used to date back in my single days were hurling copious quantities of obscene abuse that would have made a sailor blush. I found them tiresome and retorted, 'Shut up, you venomous slags!'

The Mayor of Tamworth was standing on his seat. His face was red and he was pointing his finger at me menacingly. 'You've made a mockery of my town, you filthy city slicker!' he yelled at me as I stood there ducking punches and kicks, and dodging all kinds of projectiles, including shoes, coins, phlegm and my personally autographed gold records.

Then, just as I was thinking I'd maybe been too candid about my life and times, I looked down at the other half of the crowd. In total contrast with my attackers, these folk were cheering me wildly and blowing kisses in my direction. They were a vision of love, joy and celebration, hugging each other and weeping with gratitude just for having known me. Tommy Raudonikis, Les Boyd and Bobby Cooper had tears rolling down their cheeks, which were flushed crimson by emotion and decades of alcohol abuse.

John Laws held aloft a half-empty bottle of Wild Turkey and led the crowd in a rousing rendition of 'We Are The World'.

Martin Scorsese was jumping around, excitedly repeating, 'It's gotta be a movie, man!' Bobby De Niro's face was creased into that trademark grin that seemed to say, 'Nice job, Reggie boy, nice job.' Mr T, his Mohawk now grey, was shadow-boxing with joy.

Tubby Taylor had let bygones be bygones long ago, and he was in fine spirits, considering all I'd done to him. 'You f**kin' legend!' he roared.

Oprah Winfrey had also forgiven me. She had made the trek to worship at my feet and, to my amazement, was 60 kilos lighter than the last time I saw her in Hollywood. As she cheered me, she was waving my acclaimed diet book, *Run, You Fat Prick!*, in the air, hailing it as the gospel of weight loss.

'I love you, honey. You must come back on my show!'

I yelled back at her, 'Only if you come on mine first!'

The family was there too, aunts, brothers, sisters, my kids, and then I saw her . . . standing alone, looking rapturously up at me, my Ruthie. By jeez, she was still nothing to look at, but, somehow, telling the story of my life had given me a greater appreciation of the woman she was and always will be. How could I forget the first time I took her home to meet Mum and Dad? Mum asked Ruth how long she'd been a transvestite. She said she simply couldn't believe a woman could be so ugly. Meanwhile, Dad tried to impress her by doing nude sit-ups. Ruthie took it all in her stride, just like she'd always done with my drinking and womanising. Nope, this little woman had a friggin' heart as big as Phar Lap and an arse to match.

There was nothing else to do but run to her side. I embraced her and my children cuddled in tight as well.

Lawsy immediately sensed that this was a momentous and historic occasion and, in his deep, honey-dripping voice, sang 'Love Is A Battlefield'.

My family and I were in our own little world, not hearing the cheers of my fans and supporters, and oblivious to the bottles and spit that my enemies were raining down upon us.

Then I felt a hand on my back, the same hand that had roused me from my physiotherapy session at A Touch Of

Class just a couple of hours before. Mike Munro stood there, crying like a schoolgirl. 'Reg,' he said, 'yours is the greatest story since the Bible.'

Seeing Mr T, I pulled him into the family huddle. For a brief moment the star knew what it was like to be a Reagan. Ruthie was giving the big bastard the best reverse hand job these old eyes had ever seen.

At that moment I realised I wouldn't change my life for anything or anyone in the world. I'm Reg Reagan! Go and get stuffed!!!